The Teacher's Concise Guide to

Functional
Behavioral
Assessment

The Teacher's Concise Guide to

Functional
Behavioral
Assessment

Raymond J. Waller

CORWIN PRESS
A SAGE Company

For information:

Corwin Press
A SAGE Company
2455 Teller Road
Thousand Oaks, California 91320
www.corwinpress.com

SAGE Ltd.
1 Oliver's Yard
55 City Road
London EC1Y 1SP
United Kingdom

SAGE India Pvt. Ltd.
B 1/I 1 Mohan Cooperative
Industrial Area
Mathura Road, New Delhi 110 044
India

SAGE Asia-Pacific Pte. Ltd.
33 Pekin Street #02-01
Far East Square
Singapore 048763

Printed in the United States of America

Library of Congress Cataloging-in-Publication Data

Waller, Raymond J.
The teacher's concise guide to functional behavioral assessment / Raymond J. Waller.
    p. cm.
Includes bibliographical references and index.
ISBN 978-1-4129-6604-7 (cloth)
ISBN 978-1-4129-6605-4 (pbk.)
    1. Behavioral assessment of children—United States—Handbooks, manuals, etc.
2. Behavior modification—United States—Handbooks, manuals, etc. 3. Behavior disorders in children—United States—Handbooks, manuals, etc. I. Title.

LB1124.W355 2009
370.15'28—dc22   2008034489

This book is printed on acid-free paper.

09   10   11   12   13   10   9   8   7   6   5   4   3   2   1

Acquisitions Editor:	Jessica Allan
Editorial Assistant:	Joanna Coelho
Production Editor:	Jane Haenel
Copy Editor:	Amy Rosenstein
Typesetter:	C&M Digitals (P) Ltd.
Proofreader:	Marleis Roberts
Indexer:	Michael Ferreira
Cover and Graphic Designer:	Karine Hovsepian

Contents

Acknowledgments

C orwin Press would like to gratefully acknowledge the following peer reviewers for their editorial insight and guidance in the writing of this book:

Nancy L. Cook
Associate Professor of
  Education
Hope College
Holland, MI

Debi Gartland, PhD
Professor of Special Education
Towson University
Towson, MD

Mari Gates
Educator
Henry B. Burkland School
Middleboro, MA

John M. Hintze, PhD
Professor of School Psychology
University of Massachusetts
Amherst, MA

Ramona Marquez
Director of Special Education
Hatch Valley Public Schools
Hatch, NM

Sandra Smith, PhD
Teacher
Sequim School District
Sequim, WA

Jacqueline Thousand
Professor
California State University,
San Marcos
San Marcos, CA

J. Coltrane Wolfe, PhD
Director of Special Education
Staunton City Public Schools
Staunton, VA

About the Author

 **Raymond J. Waller** is an associate professor of special education at Piedmont College and is on faculty at the University of Georgia in the School of Social Work. He is an active school consultant and trainer in the areas of severe behavior problems and child and adolescent mental health issues, a licensed clinical social worker, and a Board Certified Expert in School Crisis Response. In his spare time he practices, but has failed to master, age-appropriate social skills.

*For Katie, Sarah, Emily, Lilly Bit, Sandy, and even
Bumpus, because it doesn't get any better than that.*

CHAPTER ONE

Why FBA?

POLICY BACKGROUND

Federal law and public opinions regarding the quality of public school education have resulted in new pressures on teachers to be *accountable*. If the responsibility of educating a large group of other peoples' children does not make you feel accountable already, federal law emphasizes that teachers should be "highly qualified" to teach the material that they present in the classroom. President George W. Bush conferred his concern about education and the performance of educators to the nation with the statement, "Rarely is the question asked, 'Is our children learning?'" After a great deal of personal reflection and in the name of academic integrity, I am forced to admit that I have never heard that question asked.

Prime-time newscasts, in their capacity as the voice of a free democracy, assumed and broadened the President's education campaign, though less eloquently, on a daily basis unless more compelling news about Britney Spears demanded the nation's attention. Most teachers I have met very much feel their responsibility of teaching children; I don't think that educators' not taking the job seriously is a legitimate concern. As a person who teaches teachers and spends a good deal of time in schools, I have never met a teacher who did not believe that she should be accountable for competent job performance and highly qualified to teach her content area. I have met teachers who do not think that standardized test scores are a good reflection of their competence. This is good because the teachers who feel this way are correct.

However, the field of education, from college teacher education programs all the way to individual classrooms and students, has accommodated this legal requirement by apportioning a huge financial and intellectual investment toward ensuring that teachers are highly qualified. It is, after all, the law. As with most mandates, among the outcomes observed there were *unintended consequences* as well as *intended consequences*. One of the unintended consequences is that fewer intellectual and financial resources became available to help teachers with the issue of challenging classroom behavior. Not surprisingly, professionals working in schools, when expressing what they feel that they need help with, do not generally specify academic content. Between college teacher preparation programs, in-services, and other professional growth opportunities, most teachers express confidence about being prepared to effectively teach their content area. It is hard to graduate from a teacher education program to teach mathematics if you, for example, cannot add.

WHO IS REALLY AT FAULT IF THEY HATE SCHOOL?

Responsibility for children's negative attitudes concerning school rests entirely on our shoulders. In addition to the frequent public derision directed at schools and teachers mentioned above, we, through a variety of words and actions, sometimes convey the idea that children, frankly, just are not very bright—so they must need stricter curriculum requirements and more testing. Ironically, on television I recently saw a documentary that lasted for one entire hour (except for titillating commercial breaks), and this entire one-hour documentary was about how smart rats are getting.

If you missed this documentary, the basic message was that, at the rate at which rat intelligence is burgeoning, within weeks of this very day, your average roof rat will have an intelligence quotient (IQ) that makes Stuart Little look like Forrest Gump. Our children are getting dumber, but our rats are getting smarter? Many current messages, policies, and societal forces are creating an atmosphere that facilitates school disengagement. However, we can be the instruments of establishing school engagement with positive approaches to behavior management and by promoting the mental health of our students.

Though policy certainly affects behavior, it cannot trump the power of personal interaction and other things that you bring to your students. It is what you bring to the classroom that is most likely to engage (or disengage) your students with the school environment. The way that you teach will excite students or will bore them. You will infuse their interests in teaching, or the curriculum will be meaningless. You will say, do, and plan the things you do within the framework of promoting student mental health, or the school will become another risk factor for some students. Your approach to behavior change will promote learning and foster engagement, or it will favor some students over others.

ACADEMICS OR BEHAVIOR?

I hear teachers and administrators express a great deal of frustration about the difficult behaviors that they are seeing in schools, and they often articulate their need for assistance in dealing with student behavioral problems. This is not really surprising, considering that you, if you went through a teacher training program to become a math teacher, had many classes, not just in the subject matter, but also in what we often call "methods courses." These courses are designed to prepare you to not simply know your content area but to provide you with sound strategies on how to best teach your content area. By contrast, my guess is that it is unlikely that you took more than one or two classes on how to most effectively deal with student behavioral issues, and there is a decent chance that these classes only covered general classroom management strategies. When you consider that each child is entirely different from every other student— and that therefore the range of behaviors that you may see in the classroom is virtually unlimited—these one or two classes in behavior management are almost certainly, over the course of a teaching career, going to prove inadequate.

The encouraging news is that there are extremely good research- and practice-based strategies available to effectively and unobtrusively address the majority of behavioral problems that will arise in the classroom. In fact, most of the time such problems will respond to positive strategies, and you will not need to resort to some common, punitive approaches seen in many schools. Because of a different federal law than the one alluded to above, the Individuals with

Disabilities Education Improvement Act of 2004, one of the techniques that we must use under certain circumstances when a child receives special education services and that we should use any time a child in our class has a behavioral problem not responding to our classroom behavior management plan is a data collection process known as "functional behavior assessment," or FBA. From the information collected doing an FBA, we can then develop a function-based behavior intervention plan (BIP) with a very good chance of helping reduce or eliminate student problem behaviors. The purpose of this book is to provide you with an introduction into FBA and behavior intervention (also referred to frequently and interchangeably as "support") planning.

FBA is a term that you have probably heard if you are a teacher or if you work with children in any capacity in which their behavior is an issue. Behavior is usually thought of as anything observable and measurable that a person does. Using this definition, any place that we find children, we are likely concerned about their behavior, because a lack of behavior would suggest that the youths we are working with are not, say, breathing. As a teacher, as a child mental health worker in numerous settings, and as a school consultant for students with severe behavior problems, I have conducted and reviewed numerous approaches to assessment and to intervention planning for children with an almost unbelievable array of behavioral issues. I prefer FBA to all other types of assessment because the focus and outcome of data collection directly lead to developing a BIP with a high probability of successfully addressing the behavior problem we observe.

Common School Assessment Data

If you are familiar with typical psychological assessments such as those sometimes found in a child's school record, you know this evaluation is a document that discusses tests and testing techniques, which takes up numerous typewritten pages before summarizing the interpretation of results. Suppose, for example, that Peanut (who has the perfect kid's name) is in your classroom, but that he engages in a high rate of out-of-seat behavior and verbal calling out. These undesirable behaviors have not been eliminated by your classroom management plan, and you need to formulate a new strategy. Wanting information that could prove helpful to this process, you review Peanut's psychological evaluation, and the summary looks something like:

Axis 1: Attention deficit hyperactivity disorder (ADHD). Rule out oppositional defiant disorder.

Axis 2: None.

Axis 3: Highly allergic to peanuts (note the irony).

Axis 4: Recent parental separation.

Axis 5: Global Assessment of Functioning (GAF) 70.

Full-scale IQ 113.

The question that I have, and that you most likely share, is, "What does this information provide that will help me develop a successful plan for reducing Peanut's out-of-seat and calling-out behaviors in my classroom?" You might be enticed into responding, "Well, Peanut has a diagnosis of ADHD, so he needs to be on medication." Maybe Peanut does. However, just knowing that Peanut has a diagnosis of ADHD is not nearly enough information to be confident that medication is the answer to his behavioral issues in your classroom. In fact, medication may be more helpful for students with ADHD in the area of executive functioning than it is in the area of reducing problem behaviors. Executive functioning refers to higher order thinking skills (such as organizational skills or goal-attainment strategies) that can provide challenges to students diagnosed with ADHD—even if they are being treated with medication.

For example, I taught a student who had been diagnosed with ADHD and was being treated with medication who did not just have deficits in organizational skills—he completely lacked them. As a result and by necessity, every morning when he arrived at school, we would clean out and organize his book bag. The array of contents we culled daily would have amazed you. His book bag would slenderize from the preclean size of a fully grown tom turkey to being a mesh container that could be slid under the noise tolerance level of most principals. Every afternoon we would have to do the exact same thing again. Because he had been on school grounds all day rather than having the opportunity to free range, the diversity of contents in his book bag was dramatically reduced, even if the mass was comparable. Only on one afternoon did I find a creature that was either living or had once been alive. Instead, his overflowing afternoon book bag contained primarily papers, broken pencils, the tops of dry-erase markers, and the occasional wad of chewed gum (and I never sought the owner, fearing it would not be his).

Beyond these limitations to the efficacy of medication on the impact of symptoms often associated with ADHD is that, unless you are a school teacher who also happens to be a licensed physician, you can't write prescriptions anyway. If you can write prescriptions, you are undoubtedly popular in the teachers lounge.

The psychological data provided in the report also encourage us to rule out oppositional defiant disorder. Is that your job as a teacher? How do you go about ruling out oppositional defiant disorder? Is that even associated with out-of-seat behavior? You have no idea? This brings us back to square one. Going down the diagnostic summary further, and assuming that an allergy to peanuts is not affecting his ability to maintain in-seat behavior, we see that Peanut comes from a home that is experiencing marital stress and parental separation. Poor Peanut is obviously calling out in class in an unconscious effort to call out to the missing caregiver. He is probably jumping out of his seat in a subconscious effort to go to the missing caregiver. So here is a question: even if this interpretation of his behavior is true—and I'm not remotely implying that it is—what possible help does the information provide in helping with useful intervention planning for out-of-seat or calling-out behaviors? Maybe you should simply be sympathetic to poor Peanut and his recent family loss—whatever loss that is. Maybe right now Peanut (Mr. Peanut to acquaintances) just needs compassion, and our compassionate inner voice tells us that we should ignore his disruptive behavior.

CAUTION: CONJECTURE AHEAD!

Maybe. But such conclusions involve our making a lot of assumptions about Peanut and his family. We don't even know the circumstances of the parental separation. It could simply be a time-limited, work-related separation. And if we extend our compassion to Peanut as a primary intervention, what do we do if Peanut's classroom behavior doesn't change or if it begins to worsen? What if he starts tearing up school property? Do we still use compassion as our intervention, maybe just give more compassion? Or does tearing up school property concern us or annoy us enough to override our sympathy? I think that compassion is an emotional response we should experience when any of our students is having difficulties—but compassion is not an intervention.

Several years ago, I was asked to consult in the case of a fourth-grade girl who had hit a classmate toward the end of the school year. She was very bright and was known as a good student, and she had a history of excellent behavior at school. Extremely important and of significant concern to some of the school personnel was that two years previously, this girl had been in bed with her mother when a former boyfriend of the mother opened the bedroom window and shot her mother to death as the poor girl watched. The people at the school were quite attuned to awaiting the behavioral problems that this girl would surely have—and here they were. The trauma of the terrible event finally presented itself in the form of this fourth-grade child hitting a classmate.

I observed the classroom and talked to both students—the alleged hitter and the alleged hittee. I talked to the teachers who knew both girls. The picture that emerged was one of a year-long verbal back-and-forth that had escalated to both girls hitting each other in the classroom, but with only one getting caught. It was the terrible trauma the girl had experienced that some in the school had seized upon to explain seemingly meaningless and unprovoked aggression. I recommended that the teacher change the seating arrangement so that the two girls could no longer needle (or reach) one another. The school personnel were highly skeptical of this suggestion but finally consented to give it a try. There were no more problems reported between the girls during the school year.

I am not for a moment suggesting that the girl had not experienced a horrible, traumatic event. My point is that the trauma she had experienced may have borne no relationship whatsoever to her hitting another child in class. In fact, expecting and probing for a deep mental health explanation for every behavior problem we see is like a dentist probing for cavities with a power drill—you might cause more pain and trouble than you alleviate. This leaves us with two options: we can start probing this girl and other students like a dentist with a drill, attempting to find sensitive areas of the child's psyche that we can use to explain any undesirable behavior—maybe creating such sensitive areas where they didn't previously exist—or we can start with simple solutions first. Actually, we only have one choice because it is not a teacher's job to try to provide psychotherapy for severe psychological trauma. Am I suggesting that the girl in the case above had not experienced an unimaginably terrible event? Absolutely not. Am I suggesting that the girl had not, did not, or would never need specialized help to deal with a horrible trauma that most of us could never imagine? Absolutely not. I am, however, suggesting that the problem seen in the classroom may not have been related to the terrible event at all, and sometimes the simplest solution is the best—and maybe the only—option we have for helping in our students.

Moving yet further down the diagnostic list, we see that Peanut has a GAF of 70. However, we have no clue what a GAF is, let alone whether 70 is a good GAF or a bad GAF, so this information doesn't help at all. Finally, we see that Peanut has an IQ of 113. This tells us that Peanut is a rather bright young man, and that with his level of intelligence, he should certainly be able to understand verbal instructions. However, we have already been telling Peanut to sit down and to raise his hand before speaking, and these strategies do not seem to have helped at all. Peanut is smart enough to understand what we have told him but he still hasn't followed our directions—so maybe—make that probably, Peanut is just bad, manipulative, or noncompliant. He is flawed in some way that perhaps special education services—or maybe the juvenile justice system—can help.

Your review of the psychological information may have been slightly different than the one discussed above but, my guess is, not by much. The data have coaxed us to make assumptions about Peanut that may or may not be correct. We have a diagnosis—ADHD—that could give us the supposition that we understand why Peanut is calling out in class and doesn't remain in his seat, but we have no way of knowing at this point if our assumptions are remotely correct. Our options for intervention planning with the data available from typical assessments seem to be limited to compassion, medication, or acquisition of special education services; all of these options are based on assumptions. Two of the three are even beyond our ability to determine. In other words, any intervention plan that we develop at this point is something that we, in essence, pull out of the air. FBA provides information that is much more useful for intervention planning than typical assessment data.

CAVEAT EMPTOR: MY ASSUMPTION

Before moving forward, it is only fair that I tell you my assumption because I just urged you to make none. If you are going to be involved in the lives of children, particularly if you are going to be trying to influence their lives, you must work with them. You can't read a book to or baby-sit your niece a few times each month and expect to understand children and their needs. You must spend time with them—lots of it. Banish the myth of quality time from your vocabulary. You have to play with them, work with them, wipe their noses, and clean up their messes. When beginning my professional experience working with children, I used to be asked occasionally by parents, "So, uh, doc, do you have children?" And that question really annoyed me. Do they think their physician needs to have the flu in order to treat someone else's?

I understand their question now especially because now I do have children. In a classroom one morning, a kindergarten girl with a moderate level of cognitive impairment looked up from an art activity that had held her attention for the past several minutes and said, "Well damn! I done pissed my pants." Then she went right back to the activity. What would you do and assume if this occurred in your room? Would you think she needed toilet training? What other thoughts do you have? What kind of intervention is needed?

My thought is that this girl, like any child might do, became so occupied with what she was doing that she didn't respond to the cues her body sent her regarding her need to toilet. My thought about intervention is that the teacher may want to be careful to program bathroom breaks for her class, but nothing else (except, of course, helping the girl get cleaned up and not drawing the attention of other students to the accident—AND wishing that this girl was not exposed to words like "damn"). Do not take this as the suggestion to go forth and procreate, unless of course you were already planning to. Keep in mind, though, that FBA and BIP are advanced stuff, and undertaking them assumes that you already have a good background working with children.

WHAT'S NOT TO LIKE? REASONS I LIKE FBA

FBA Is Not Diagnostic

When thinking about student behavior and student behavior problems, educators function beneath two broad identifying categories: *labels* and *diagnoses*. A child, as a result of various data sources and professional decisions and opinions, may be given a school label based on federal or state criteria that connote a disability category negatively impacting a student's learning. Labels such as *emotional/behavior disorder* and *other health impairment* may apply to students who meet specific eligibility criteria. These labels then—if determined by an interdisciplinary team, including the child's caregiver, to adversely affect learning—may qualify a student for an *individualized educational plan (IEP)*, in which modifications and accommodations to the learning environment and to curricular materials are described. The stipulations of an IEP essentially constitute a contractual agreement and are legally binding between adult caregivers and a school system about accommodations and modifications that a child will receive to address educational needs impairing a student from academically progressing.

Diagnoses, on the other hand, relate to mental health categories and specific mental illness conditions that a person may experience. Diagnoses are made by qualified mental health professionals such as clinical social workers, psychologists, and psychiatrists (physicians who specialize in mental health) and sometimes by physicians in general, internal, and pediatric practice. The most common diagnostic reference tool used in the United States for mental health issues is the *Diagnostic and Statistical Manual of Mental Health Disorders, Fourth Edition, Text Revision* (DSM-IV-TR). As a highly trained mental health professional, diagnoses are helpful to me for the following reasons:

1. Diagnoses provide a frame of reference, such that if I am told that a child is experiencing major depressive disorder, I know that the child is experiencing five of nine symptoms outlined for major depressive disorder by the DSM-IV-TR and that these symptoms have been present for at least two weeks. This gives me an intellectual short cut in conceptualization and treatment planning and can be useful shorthand for research purposes.

2. If I diagnose a child with a specific disorder from the DSM-IV-TR, then I can bill the child's medical insurance for treatment (if she has any).

These advantages of labels and diagnoses (and let's not understate the whole "bill insurance" thing), however, must be weighed against several known disadvantages. First and foremost, it is absolutely clear that labeling or diagnosing children can have a negative impact resulting from the stigma often associated with these very labels and diagnoses. This is not just one of those statements that are popped off commonly for fun— abundant research has been consistent on identifying the negative impact of labeling and diagnosing children. What's more, if you identify a child as a behavior problem in kindergarten, there will be people who tend to regard that student as a behavior problem years later, regardless of how she behaves.

Assigning labels and diagnoses can also lead people to infer that they understand a child, even though they do not. Considering the example of major depressive disorder listed above, can you name the nine symptoms? If not, then you may have a mental image of what depression is. Unfortunately that image may well be incorrect because the way that depression manifests in children can dramatically differ from what we usually think of as depression as seen in adults. If you can name the nine symptoms, you probably need to broaden your social horizons dramatically or find a comforting hobby. I can name them, by the way, which should tell you a great deal about me. It is vital to remember at all times that a person is more than the sum of their labels and diagnoses. I have *never* read a child's chart and felt like I knew or understood her. In fact, on several occasions I have been told horror stories about a child that was going to be coming to my class or that I was going to be working with, and then I never had any trouble with her. I am sure that you have either had a similar situation or you will have a similar situation. I like to refer all rumor mongers about a new student to Waller's First Rule of Child Behavior Management: *You don't know until they show.*

So there tends to be a lot of bias, stigma, and misinformation surrounding labels and diagnoses. My oldest daughter came home from school one day in a state of emotional arousal that I can best describe with the term tizzy (as of her 13th birthday, she comes home MOST days in a tizzy). I asked her why she was in said tizzy, and she told me that she had passed a church sign that really bothered her. We rode over to take a look and took a picture of it.

She wanted to write a letter to the editor of our local newspaper and to the pastor of the church expressing her dismay at

Source: Sarah E. Waller.

what the sign implied. Although I discouraged her from pursuing that course of action, I could see her point. If you consider the slogan for a minute, you may or may not see the implication's relation to depression—but at least contemplate the irony that descriptions of depression go back at least as far as—and are actually described in—the Bible. She intuitively has a sense of Waller's Second Rule of Child Behavior Management: *If it walks like a duck and quacks like a duck, it's not abnormal just because it's a parakeet.*

Respect and Dignity

Related to the issue of stigma associated with labels is yet another reason that I am preferential to FBA. FBA is a respectful process to a child. Undesirable behaviors, from the standpoint of doing an FBA, are understood to serve a specific function (or purpose). In other words, behaviors occur because they work for a student in some way or in some setting. Think about it—if you engaged in a behavior that served no purpose, you would stop doing that behavior. Conceptually then, our goal in doing an FBA is to gather information that will help us develop a hypothesis about a targeted behavior of concern, from which we can develop an intervention to

- change the circumstances associated with an undesirable behavior, and/or
- teach a desirable alternate behavior that can provide the outcome of the undesired behavior, thereby
- eliminating the temptation to think of a child as bad or flawed in some way.

In fact, it seems to me that sometimes we use labels as a means to avoid intervening, rather than to help us with effective intervention planning, as represented by exchanges like:

"How could he possibly have stolen her pencil?"

"He's conduct disordered."

"How do you know he's conduct disordered?"

"Because conduct disordered kids steal."

"Ohhhhh."

Solid Grounding in Research

FBA and function-based intervention planning is not an educational fad— these approaches are undergirded by solid research that has been accumulating for decades. It seems that periodically, in the field of education, some new plan, strategy, or theory becomes popular and is marketed in such a way as to imply that this plan or strategy is *the* answer to whatever problems we might be seeing in schools, despite the truth of Waller's Third Rule of Child Behavior Management: *When talking about human behavior, NO strategy works all of the time or for every student, and anyone that tells you otherwise is probably trying to sell you something.*

There are, however, hundreds and hundreds of published accounts of successful intervention plans based on FBAs available in the professional literature. I teach a graduate-level class on FBA in which the primary requirement is that my students conduct an FBA, develop a function-based intervention, and implement the plan. I have supervised more than a hundred teachers who have conducted FBAs on target behaviors ranging from self-injurious head strikes, to masturbation, to simple talking out in class, and I can recall only one intervention that did not result in substantial, if not total, resolution of the problem behavior. In my class, I do not grade on whether or not the intervention works, only on the process of doing the FBA, the logic of the intervention plan, and the way the plan was implemented. I want my graduate students to be willing to try to target challenging behaviors, not pick simple problems just because they have a good chance of developing an intervention plan that works. People may be skeptics about FBA when they begin the course, but I haven't seen a teacher yet that was a skeptic 16 weeks later, because they then understand Waller's Fourth Rule of Child Behavior Management: *Your best intentions can never replace your best efforts, the usefulness of which depend on the information directing these efforts.*

The Focus of Change

Finally, I prefer FBA to other assessment methods for addressing undesirable classroom behavior because the data are directly applicable to intervention planning and the focus of the intervention is *what we do differently* rather than *what we do to a child*. That is not in any way intended to imply that we try to find something that was done wrong by somebody, such as another teacher or a parent. Blame assignment is a popular method often used when problematic school behaviors or national debates occur, even though I have never seen blame assignment resolve even the simplest behavior issue.

The goal of support planning based on FBA is to strategize about what can be done differently to increase the odds of seeing desirable behavior. There are some people who see behavior intervention planning as a sequence of things we do to a student in order to make them do what we want, typically by punishing them for things that they do that we don't want them to do. Such an approach often involves a hierarchy or sequence of things we do to children that are designed to get more unpleasant with successive occurrences of undesirable behavior. In fact, I have seen documents called BIPs that looked something like this:

River Styx Primary School
Behavior Intervention Plan

Progressive Corrective Action Form
Please note the behavior demonstrated and the corrective action applied.
Include any further information below.

Student Name:_____ Date:_____

o Verbal Reprimand	o Detention
o Punch License	o In-School Suspension
o Time Out/Letter Home	o Corporal Punishment
o Office Referral	o Out-of-School Suspension

NOTES:
_____
_____
_____
_____
_____

Teacher Name:_____

Teacher Signature:_____ Date:_____

Administrator Signature:_____ Date:_____

Do yourself a favor: if your school has a BIP that looks remotely similar to this, don't bother doing an FBA. It will be a complete waste of time because forms like this do not constitute a BIP, nor are they conducive to doing a BIP. This is just a list of increasingly objectionable things that you will do to a student who doesn't do what you desire. If we feel tempted to do unpleasant things to children because they deserve it, we do need to face a hard truth, however, that doing something to a student frequently has no positive effect and can easily make things worse than they were before. At the very least, when attempting to intervention plan, have perspective enough to think in terms of cause and effect. If your attempts to punish away undesirable behavior have not worked, it's time to consider a different approach.

REASONS YOU WILL LIKE FBA

Avoid Failing at Social Control

It is worth your time to reflect deeply on personal philosophy relating to your thoughts regarding the purpose of the school experience in the lives of children and to think about your role in the school community. A lot of adults, including some teachers, perceive their role in the lives of children, at least as it pertains to behavioral issues, as agents of social control. In other words, some people impose, or try to impose, their will onto students—sometimes on other adults, too. We sometimes are tempted to think that our role as a teacher (or administrator), combined with our adulthood, instills us with authority that must be respected by our students. We don't need no stinking badges—your authority is obvious to all by virtue of the fact that you have a faculty parking spot and are wearing an old tie.

In fact, this is only partially true—the tie is somewhat dated. We do, nonetheless, have authority and you are the adult and your tie was last in fashion when the artistic style preferred by the popular culture was called hieroglyphics. However, you only have *coercive* authority as long as your students allow you to have it, and using coercive authority is contrary to acquisition of academic content and to promoting a positive learning environment. Coercive authority relates to the idea that children will, by golly, do what you tell them to do because you, by cracky, told them to do it.

Fortunately for disciplinarians who prefer coercive approaches like threats and punishment, many students, actually most of them, will allow you to have coercive authority, at least to an extent. Most students will roll with the flow and make an effort to do what you ask. Some number of additional students will pretend to let you have authority, but will be sneaking around doing things that you would prefer that they not do. In fact, this gives children a good opportunity to hone their "sneaking around doing stuff behind your back" skills so that by the time they are in third grade they are bringing cake to you in the morning and putting wads of chewed cafeteria chicken product in your purse in the afternoon—without ever getting caught.

A smaller group of students will blatantly resist or defy direct coercive authority. I was observing a third-grade classroom, and a girl was giving the teacher fits. She seemed to know every button to push and was defying verbal instructions. Finally, the teacher called the office and asked for assistance. The assistant principal, a coach-looking guy who was new to the school, walked over to the student and said in a stern voice while flashing "the eye of the tiger" at the girl, "Get up and come with me." The little girl looked at the hulking assistant principal sweetly and said, "Kiss my ass." I will remember the look on his face for the rest of my life.

Whenever you begin to use coercive authority as a mechanism of behavior change, you immediately start to descend a slippery slope. If you enter into a power struggle with a student having behavioral problems, the odds are about 50/50 that you will lose (and about 80% that both of you will lose). If you forcefully tell a student to stop talking and the student begins to sing a pop song, what are you going to do? Now you have a noncompliant student and the repulsive prospect of listening to a song that is not at least 25 years old. Furthermore, getting into coercive exchanges or power struggles has been shown to directly cause some problems—a good example being the oppositional defiant disorder that was mentioned earlier.

If you demand that a student goes to timeout and the student gets up and sits in your chair, what are you going to do? Making demands on students only works if the student allows it to work or if you have the will and the means to oblige your will upon the student. As the associate principal described above found out, the hint of threat suggested by a burly, strapping school administrator with a predatory look and a crew cut is, by itself, sometimes insufficient to resolve a behavior problem. He wound up being one of three adults that it took to physically remove this third-grade student from the classroom. The end result was that the entire class lost more than 30 minutes of instruction as the drama played itself out, four other students in the classroom started to cry because the episode scared them so badly, and the little girl came back one hour later, placed her head on her desk, and left it there for the rest of the day.

You Can Do This

Teachers are working more than they ever have in the past. I will not lie to you by saying that there is no time involved in the process of doing an FBA. When schools call me and request that I do an FBA on a consultative basis, it usually takes me 20 to 25 hours. But, as a consultant, I have to be extremely thorough and write a report that is usually about 10 pages long and those 20 hours include attending (sometimes contentious) IEP meetings. In fact, it was during one such meeting that I clearly articulated in my mind the definition of a good day: If you are in a roomful of people, at least 20% of whom are attorneys, and one person leaves the room without crying and that one person is you, then you have had a good day.

Also, schools don't call me when Peanut is annoyingly tapping his pencil on his desk. I usually get called when there are serious behavior problems. My consultation work literally began when a school administrator that I didn't know called me out of the blue and asked if I would come to her school and help with a particularly problematic behavior. This experience gave me some idea of the level of need that exists in helping students with behavior problems. Schools need you to have the skills to do this. Successfully resolving the majority of behavior problems seen in schools is easily within the purview of a skill set that any teacher can acquire with a little help. Besides the professional obligation to maintain classroom behavior conducive to learning, many of us find that successful intervention planning for a student with challenging behavior—particularly a student with a history of challenging behavior—has the personal effect of instilling in us a level of satisfaction and excitement that we otherwise experience exclusively in response to undergoing videotaped exploratory medical procedures. Life simply gets no better. The professional contribution you have made in that student's life at least competes with the contribution of any academic content you will teach him.

There is an important point about people like me consulting in schools, though, and it is this: *every dollar spent on me as a consultant is a dollar that is NOT being spent on other students* (and please don't tell anybody I told you this because I'm sure it's a violation of the Consultant's Creed or something, but I have that whole "full-time job thing" as a financial buffer). Most FBAs could be done by you and could be done in much less time than it takes me to do it for reasons that I already touched on and some reasons that will become obvious in subsequent chapters. I promise you—even pinky promise—that you can do an FBA.

I also do training for schools on child mental health issues, behavior management, FBA, and talking about where FBA fits into the response to intervention (RTI) paradigm (and please don't tell anyone else how to do an FBA because training comes out of a different budget that schools are required to spend exclusively on training, so I don't feel guilty at all about getting paid for doing training), but an FBA and subsequent BIP can and should be done long before special education services (the point at which FBA can be required by law) are even considered. In other words, more and more of this is going to be done in the general classroom. Don't blame me—it's not my fault. Don't hate the player, hate the game. And even though there is a time investment needed up front, the student will benefit tremendously.

I hope that supports are put in place to help you with FBA from a variety of sources such as paraeducators, other teachers, administrators, school social workers, school psychologists, and school counselors. But keep this in mind: every hour you invest in doing an FBA and function-based BIP now will ultimately save a lot of time that you won't be spending by dealing with behavior problems later. Trust me on this. However, you need to never forget Waller's Fifth Rule of Child Behavior Management: *"Congressman" is a job: Working with children is a commitment and lifestyle that means never counting the hours you invest.*

ADDRESSING MY LIFE

I know that the title of this book includes the word *concise* and hints that the book is, among other things, nontechnical. That is a lie. There are actually a couple of technical terms that will be of assistance, maybe even be indispensible, in understanding the FBA process. The first such term is *reinforcement.* We hear the word frequently in the school setting, but there is often some confusion about what it means. Reinforcement, by definition, is something that increases a *target behavior* (another term you need to know).

The Good, the Bad, and the Not-So-Punishing

For discussion purposes, let's say you are working with a student who is frequently out of his seat rather than engaging in the academic tasks that you want him to be focusing on. Each time the student (Peanut) gets out of his seat (the target behavior), you give him a stern warning (an attempt to reduce or punish the target behavior). You notice, because you carefully observe the order in which things happen (cause and effect) that after you started giving Peanut stern reprimands for getting out of his seat, he seemed to start getting out of his seat more often. Even though your goal and intention was to reduce Peanut's out-of-seat behavior, your intervention increased his out-of-seat behavior. In other words, your warnings and reprimands *reinforced* his out-of-seat behavior. This may not seem intuitive. After all, you don't like stern reprimands, so it is reasonable to think that Peanut will stop getting out of his seat if you reprimand him.

Unreasonable though it may seem, your reprimands *reinforced* Peanut's out-of-seat behavior, even if he found them unpleasant. Your disapproval may have reduced Peanut to crying like a monkey eating a red onion, but your reprimands nonetheless reinforced (increased) the target behavior. You intended to reduce it (or punish it), but it is very important that you realize that behavior may not seem reasonable or intuitive. If you doubt this, pay attention during your next faculty meeting.

Not only is human behavior often illogical, reinforcement is *not an intuitive term, it is a behavioral term.* Thus, something is reinforcing if it increases a target behavior. In Peanut's case, he may have found the reprimands unpleasant, but they still increased the target behavior. The point of this is that you cannot rationally, reasonably, and with common sense identify reinforcers (or things that will increase an identified target behavior) for a given student. Reinforcers are determined on the basis of the *impact that they have on a target behavior,* not on how pleasant or even how desirable the reinforcer may seem. Similarly, reinforcers used effectively for your other students are in no way guaranteed to work for Peanut.

It may also help to understand the seeming contradiction that reprimands resulted in more of the target behavior to know another idea associated with reinforcement: you don't reinforce a person, you reinforce a behavior. Even if your reprimands were unpleasant to Peanut, they reinforced out-of-seat behavior. This explains why the offer of watching a movie on Friday based on good behavior all week is often completely insufficient in promoting the various behaviors you desire. This is an attempt, at least in behavioral terms, to reinforce a week-long repertoire of innumerable behaviors with one potential reinforcer. Reinforcement is not accomplished by picking untold numbers of behaviors, lumping them together so that they are as unattractive as homemade soup, and providing one reinforcer for successfully engaging in the behavioral package. Much behavior, especially undesirable behavior—especially in children—must be reinforced far more frequently than once a week anyway. Offering a large weekly reinforcer contingent on desired behavioral goals that a student does not already possess with mastery is literally setting him up to fail every week, week after week.

You may have noted above, for example, that I mentioned a school administrator calling me out of the blue because of the need for help with a particularly problematic behavior, not a particularly problematic child. The path to developing problematic behavior is very similar for any child, and any child is susceptible to acquiring undesirable behavior under the right circumstances as surely as she can develop desirable behavior. The good news associated with this is that, just as any child can acquire undesirable behavior, any child can acquire new, more desirable behavior if the classroom supports change in the right direction.

Target Behaviors

The idea of a *target behavior* is that you get very specific about a behavior that you want to change. For example, saying that your boss is annoying is not providing a description that is observable and that we can monitor in a meaningful way, because we don't know what you mean by annoying. A common behavior of concern in school is sometimes called unmotivated. My definition of unmotivated is the refusal to don trousers during the 48-hour period often referred to as "weekend." Your definition might be different, though if it is not, that really could be a big problem at school. Spend a couple of minutes thinking about how you might give a good, specific, clear definition of what you mean when you say unmotivated. This definition should be so clear and descriptive that, if it were being counted, would result in another person counting it just like you counted it by just their reading the definition. Write the definition below in a clear, observable, countable way:

_____

_____

_____

_____

Now think about whether or not your definition, sometimes referred to as an *operational definition*, is clear enough so that anyone walking into the room would count the behavior and get the same result you that you obtained if you counted it at the same time. See the difference in your definition and the information typically communicated by just using terms like unmotivated?

It is important to clearly define your target behavior so that everyone will be working on the same goal. You are working with Peanut to teach him an alternative, more desirable behavior than calling out in class. He has this problem of calling out in all of his classes. As part of your intervention plan, Peanut is on a simple point system allowing him to earn some extra computer time at the end of the day. This point system is used by each of Peanut's teachers, but the plan is one you designed based on results of an FBA. Having a clearly defined target behavior is necessary in order to keep the plan on track. Otherwise, some of Peanut's teachers, perhaps not as versed in effective behavior management as you, may count it against Peanut if engages in minor undesired behavior that is unrelated to calling out.

For example, a teacher may hold him accountable on his point sheet if he is seen leaning over and whispering to a classmate. I would not say that this type of data collection challenge occurs a lot of the time. In my personal experience, it happens almost every time you are working with several other teachers. If such unrepresentative data collection happens, it has the effect of masking evidence that your intervention is working (or not working). Holding against him things that were not part of your regular deal is also totally unfair to Peanut, and he knows it. I know Peanut well enough to tell you that, when he knows (or even suspects) he is being treated unfairly, no good is going to come of it. Knowing that such inaccuracy is likely to occur is your first step in monitoring the data; then, identifying these occurrences and working with your colleagues to repair any procedural problems is usually all that is needed to keep the intervention in place and the data collection consistent and meaningful.

A clear operational definition of the target behavior is important because you cannot keep an accurate count of the behavior otherwise. Remember the cardinal rule: the definition needs to be so clear that I could walk into your classroom, count the target behavior at the same time you do, and when finished counting for both of us to have the same number. Beyond the issue of effectiveness of the intervention, you need good data for progress monitoring purposes, particularly if your school operates within an RTI framework. RTI will be discussed in somewhat more detail later.

Accuracy is paramount, and monitoring Peanut's progress will leave you unsatisfied, not to mention potentially unsuccessful, if you don't know the true measure of what is going on. For example, how many times have you found yourself right in the middle of a major, potentially life-changing situation such as taking the SAT or watching *The Price Is Right* when unwanted and unbidden it occurs to you that you don't know how many licks it takes to get to the Tootsie Roll center of a Tootsie Pop? Pretty unsatisfying, isn't it? Fortunately, you need never get lost in the middle of calculating the values of prizes shown during the showcase showdown again. The answer, based on the results of a group of university students who built a licking machine that was designed to accurately replicate the licking power of a human tongue just to break the cultural ennui that holds us by the prostration imposed by this quandary is 364 (licks, that is, to get to the center of a Tootsie Pop). If you can tolerate a brief falter into vanity I admit to you that it is exactly this level of commitment and sacrifice to resolving the challenges facing our world that makes me proud to work in higher education.

Your Humble but Invariably Correct Perceptions

A final reason that it's important to track Peanut's progress is a point that I have learned through working with human behavior—people often do not see behavioral issues in shades of gray, only in terms of black and white. Repeatedly I find that you must teach people to see the shades of gray. If Peanut is frequently calling out in your classroom, it is annoying, distracting, and disruptive. After you conducted an FBA and developed and implemented a good function-based support plan, your data collection clearly showed a trend in reduction of the calling out. In other words, the intervention was working. However, another of Peanut's teachers comes to you a week after implementing the support plan in her room and says that the plan is not working and something drastic needs to be done.

Understandably, because calling out is so disrupting and annoying to your colleague, it is easy for her to perceive that things have not improved if Peanut is calling out in her classroom at all. This moment was made in heaven exclusively for you to whip out your data. You spend the next few minutes teaching your colleague to see behavior in shades of gray by showing your coworker the data and explaining that even though the behavior has not stopped, it is getting better, expressing your gratitude for her implementing the plan with such fidelity, conveying empathetic understanding of how disruptive calling out can be, and encouraging her to give the plan some more time. She is not antagonistic toward your plan or toward helping Peanut. She simply didn't see the gray point, which is that things are improving. Behavior is not switched off and on like a light switch. Behavior change occurs as new behaviors and skills are learned, practiced, and mastered.

When you are considering your options for whether and how to intervene with student behavior, the decision tree in Figure 1.1 is a

Figure 1.1   Response to Undesirable Behavior Decision Tree

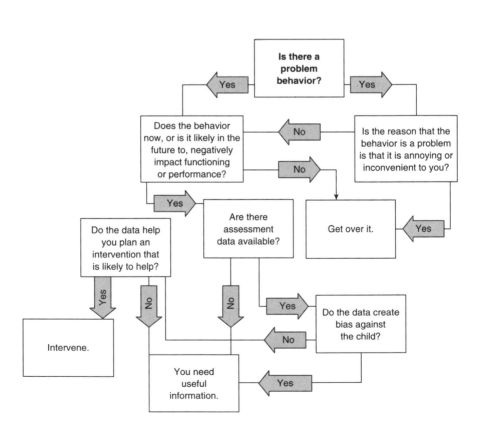

good place to begin. If you decided that you need useful information in order to proceed with developing a BIP with a high probability of success, the methods of going about collecting the type of information with the best chance of moving you toward that effective BIP are described in the following chapter.

Chapter Notes

Anyone with an interest in school activities, policies, and methods that promote student mental health may be interested in a brand-new journal that is being published:

Advances in School Mental Health Promotion: Training and Practice, Research and Policy. The Clifford Beers Foundation and the University of Maryland.

I would very much like to thank Maribeth Hood for her help and her knowledge.

CHAPTER TWO

Conjunction Junction, What's the Behavior's Function?

I have heard many explanations given for why children engage in behaviors that are undesirable to adults. "He's just like his brother (daddy, uncle, godmother, imaginary friend Pogo)," "He's just bad," "He's being manipulative," and "He's trying my nerves on purpose" are some popular explanations. Genetics, personality disorders or flaws, assuming the mother or father (or both) are frequent imbibers of crack cocaine, and expressing the firm conviction that the student in question is possessed by demons are yet other explanations of behavior problems I have heard from school personnel. In the interest of intellectual honesty, I must confess that functional behavioral assessment (FBA) has not been shown to be useful if a target behavior is the result of demonic possession.

It is certainly true that genetics play a significant role in human behavior, but even genetics, at least to an extent, are at the mercy of the environment. For example, perhaps you carry a gene that could result in your becoming an Olympic-class weight lifter under ideal circumstances and with world-class training, but rather than maximizing your Olympic weight lifting potential, you live off of the land in the middle of a virgin forest (if you can still find one). You live in such a manner, in fact, that you are offered your own television program during which, on a weekly basis, you teach survival strategies to people who need to know the survival skills associated with ordering takeout pizza; also, you dig through piles of scat and look for clues that will tell you what animal left them, and you eat bugs. Under these circumstances, genetics or not, it is unlikely that you will become an Olympic weight lifter. The other explanations mentioned above have not been found empirically to matter (or even, at least from an empirical perspective, exist). So, what are factors that are actually involved in most undesirable school behaviors?

THE REAL BEHAVIORAL CULPRITS

Research has shown that only a few things serve as the function for the majority of misbehavior at school: attention, escape, tangible items, and sensory input issues (sometimes called automatic reinforcement). Though you may see alternative lists of functions in other places that vary somewhat, the four listed above are invariably going to be on those lists and probably cover everything that you need to think about. It is not unusual for "having control" to be on a list of behavioral functions. However, if you ask yourself "Control over what?" we often get back to our listed four. For many people, thinking about behavior in terms of these four commonly identified functions represents a true paradigm shift in behavior intervention.

In education, we throw around terms like *paradigm shift* all the time without really knowing what the terms mean. Your lunch date, despite his claim, did not experience a paradigm shift when he decided to order a salad instead of a cheeseburger. He simply experienced what is referred to as a bad choice. A paradigm shift refers to a change in your worldview. Again, for many people, approaching assessment and intervention from the perspective of behavior serving a purpose instead of behavior reflecting internal inadequacies and personality flaws is a paradigm shift that is capitulated by Waller's Sixth Rule of Child Behavior Management: *Any undesirable childhood behavior can be made inefficient, ineffective, or unnecessary unless you forget that the behavior serves a purpose for that child.*

Attention

Attention is one of the most powerful phenomena that impact the development of human behavior. This point will be repeated because it is crucial. All of us have the need for interaction with and attention from others, although some few people may not seem to have the desire. In children, attention from adults is a developmental need that they must have met. If you compare our current human condition to our very distant ancestors, you will notice that, over time, as we adapted and learned, our brains grew bigger and bigger except for our brother-in-law. Other mammals are usually born with rudimentary skills necessary for survival. They have instincts, they know some creatures are friends and some are dangerous, they can swim or walk and run almost immediately after birth, so they can keep up with the herd.

Not us. Our brains got bigger and bigger. Convolutions in the brain appeared, resulting in the ability for even more brain to be wadded into our skulls. We cram a lot of brain into our skull. If you go and look into a mirror, you will probably notice that the head you see with all the brain in it is much larger than that very same head was as it left the birth canal. Our heads continue to grow long after we are born, and the brain is not completely developed until a person is in their twenties. If human babies were born with heads the size of the one you see in the mirror, I think it's safe to say that the birth rate would be drastically lower than it is and that those offspring who were born would resemble bobble heads.

The trade-off that humans make for our brains continuing to grow substantially after birth is that our newborns are much more dependent on us—and for a much longer time—than most other animals. Because of the enormous amount of growth and maturation that occurs in humans and human brains after we are born, our newborns depend on us for everything. They depend on us for their survival much longer than most of our planetary partners.

To survive, babies must be able to efficiently obtain attention from adults. Within minutes of life, they start to get our attention by crying. If hungry, afraid, thirsty, dirty, cold, scared, or maybe just bored, they will cry to get our attention. Not long thereafter their attention-getting technique has refined itself into their attempting to get our attention by consuming dust bunnies and an occasional moth. Developmentally, and to survive, children continue to need our attention and to try various methods of getting it, such that, by the time they are 13, they get our attention by ridiculously asking if they can borrow our credit card and feigning surprise when we say no. Both crying and asking to borrow our credit card are getting our attention in ways that might be described by some adults as unpleasant. Loud recordings of crying babies, in fact, is a method of acceptable torture to those who find torture acceptable.

Regardless of whether we find the mechanism by which they get our attention pleasant or unpleasant, children have a developmental need—in fact, they have a developmental mandate—to be able to get our attention as efficiently as possible, and they have that need for a very long time. Sometimes children get our attention most effectively by doing something that we find unpleasant such as moving back into our homes when they are fully grown because we foolishly neglected to change our locks or move when they left for college. In the classroom, they may get our attention in ways we find unpleasant, such as frequently calling out in class about things unrelated to the academic content being taught.

Attention is also something that children may sometimes want to avoid. For example, a kindergarten boy with an autism spectrum disorder learned that he could avoid the attention of his teacher by saying and repeating the phrase, "Smacking that ass, smacking that ass. . . ." While repeating this phrase, his right hand would begin at about shoulder height with palm facing inward, then completing a semicircle by arcing this hand in a half moon motion that drew a pattern representing a backward letter "C," then coming to an abrupt stop at the level of his waist, truly imitating the type of hand movement that one would indeed use to spur a reluctant plow mule to move onward. When he did these things in class, a paraprofessional, whose attention the boy desired a great deal, would remove him from the room and walk him around until he stopped these somewhat distracting verbalizations.

Escape

We are born with limited ability to escape. A baby can escape from something painful by twitching a limb away. We quickly acquire more ability to escape from things that are emotionally painful—things that are frightening, things that make us anxious, and things we find unpleasant. Advanced adult escape techniques include feigning illness from work so that we can go to televised sporting events featuring vehicles with large tires and mud. Escape is a common phenomenon in schools as well and can take many forms. Even extremely young children can become unreasonably and strongly avoidant (sometimes, depending on severity of avoidance, referred to as "phobic") to different things, settings, and circumstances.

Many of us have heard the famous story of Little Albert. Psychologist J. B. Watson was interested in anxiety and avoidance and set out to see if he could actually cause someone, in this case Little Albert, to be afraid of something (a white rat). Stated very simply, Little Albert was shown pictures of a white rat and, as soon as he looked at the rat, a loud bang was made behind him. When the noise was made, Little Albert would be startled, begin to cry, and attempt to move away. After combining the picture with the noise a few times, Little Albert started to cry and tried to escape from just the picture of a rat whether the noise was paired with it or not. Little Albert now escaped from the rat whenever it appeared. Not only did he escape from the rat, but he escaped from a lot of other hairy white things that had not been paired with the unpleasant noise because his fear generalized to other similar objects.

Think about this in relation to a child in the school environment. Children are taken from settings in which they often are comfortable—if for no other reason than because it is familiar to them—and know the adults and children around them. They are placed in a milieu in which they may be acquainted with nobody. They are not allowed freedom of access and freedom of choice that they have probably had before. Any of these new people, situations, or settings could cause anxiety and trigger the desire to escape. Further, by definition, children are in a place where they don't know how to do the things they are being asked to do! It is not uncommon, therefore, for students to develop a tendency to avoid numerous stimuli associated with the school environment.

Tangibles

We live in a capitalist society. We are a people that love stuff. From the time that they can process information with their sensorium, children are bombarded with words, sounds, and images, the aim of which is to convince kids that they need stuff, that they absolutely cannot live without stuff. By the time they have entered school, most children have seen thousands of advertisements and have actually already established many brand preferences. It is neither unusual nor unexpected, given our obsession with stuff, for a problem behavior to serve the purpose of giving the child access to tangible items.

Even in the school environment, children often have material needs that parents are expected to meet such as notebooks, pencils, paper, and other supply-related things. The possession of some stuff or some brands of stuff can provide more status to students with these popular brands than those students without such socially desirable things. Our societal emphasis on stuff affects our behavior in some ways that may be good but certainly in other ways that are not.

To attempt to have every student ready with all supplies they need, parents often get supply lists of the stuff that students are supposed to bring when they start school. However, some parents, whether unwilling, unaware, or unable, fail to provide supplies that teachers request that their students have. A graduate student came to me one night before class and told me that, at the school in which she taught, a bulletin board in the main hallway was dedicated to publicizing the names of students who had not brought in their listed supplies. My student told me that the teachers in the school called the bulletin board "the wall of shame." I was certain that she must be mistaken, that no responsible adult would allow such a thing, let alone create such a situation.

The next day, I called the school and found out that my student was correct and that the wall of shame stood as surely and more dramatically, at least to students in that school, as does the Wall of China. I expressed my opinion strongly about the inappropriateness of this display and was told that the wall of shame would come down immediately. Children are under more than enough pressure to meet certain standards, to see certain movies, to have a certain type of binder and book bag, and to wear brand-name clothes to easily explain why they might engage in certain behaviors to get preferred tangible items.

Sensory Stimulation

If you drive down any road, and I hope that you won't for the following reason, you will observe adults who are driving down the very same road as you while meeting their own need for sensory input in a number of ways that distract them from the task of driving; in doing so, they put themselves at risk of acquiring the sensory stimulation one receives by guiding a motorized vehicle into a tree. I have seen all manner of activities occurring in motorized vehicles, and I will only list activities that I have personally seen from drivers of moving cars: reading, singing, eating, watching DVDs, and engaging in hygiene activities that I would not want them to do in my car. Among the most interesting was a person who passed me when driving on an interstate highway while consuming a quarter section of what had recently been a large watermelon.

Multitasking in a busy world

In the constant quest for stimulation, we can watch podcasts while walking, listen to music on elevators, and I even saw television screens installed and playing away above the pumps at a local gas station. We have important family conversations with a really good movie playing in the background. At work, we can use our computers to alternate between work that we do for money and shopping-related Web surfing that we do to throw away our money while talking on the phone while listening to the radio while a peaceful personal desk-size water fountain flows behind us, its meditative trickle filling us with that Zen-like serenity that characterizes American life.

We are multitasking. Of course, we are not really multitasking. We are switching our attention from one task to the next. Our brains can only attend to one cognitive task at a time—some coworkers not even that many—but we pretend we can do many things all at the same time. It suits our fast-paced society. We are constantly bombarded with stimuli. So it comes as little surprise that among the most common behavior problems I hear teachers talk about include behaviors like pencil tapping, humming, drumming, and seat dancing. These behaviors enrich the sensory environment, with students attempting to create for themselves the raucous and unceasing sensory input that they typically experience in other settings and that your geography lesson strangely doesn't gratify.

Our children are not immune to the expectation of constant sensory input that we have created, so it is inevitable that they will sometimes, probably even frequently, engage in behaviors like the ones mentioned above. We have become stimulation junkies. Today's children are, in a sense, especially during lectures and other passive learning activities, in a state of sensory deprivation. These behaviors, however, are unpleasant or annoying to many teachers and might be considered undesirable school behaviors.

To thine own self be true

Ironically, if we place a teacher who doesn't like student pencil tapping into a room with no computer, radio, television, or handheld battery-operated poker game, with no source of sensory input besides the drone of a college professor, he will almost certainly, within minutes, begin a pattern of fidgeting that often rapidly progresses to humming, drumming, seat dancing, and pencil tapping. I know this because the teacher I'm describing is in my college classes right now.

My point here is that, believe it or not, adults have the same basic needs and responses that children have. Sometimes it helps with intervention planning to acknowledge that children doing similar things to what we might also do in similar circumstances are not lazy or distracting, they are normal. Children and adults share the same types of need and respond, whether positively or negatively, to similar stimuli. Further, I find it quite interesting that the same instructional strategies that facilitate the most learning and retention in children facilitate the same outcome for adults. Regardless of age, we are all human.

SKILLS DEFICITS IN UNDESIRABLE BEHAVIOR

A phenomenon frequently implicated in the development and maintenance of classroom behavior problems is the issue of skills deficits. Skills deficits deserve to have a discussion of their own because skills deficits are frequently associated with disruptive school behavior. As a matter of fact, it is wise to assume that the function of any disruptive behavior seen in the classroom is either correlated with skills deficits or a skills deficit was the cause of the development and is involved in the maintenance of the behavior. Skills deficits can be the seed from which any classroom behavioral problem grows. Skills deficits can synergistically impact any of the above four functions of a target behavior and worsen that target behavior.

An area of skills deficit that is intuitively associated with classroom behavioral challenges is academic skills deficits. If a child is not, for example, reading as fluently as same-aged peers, she will quickly find herself behind in this instructional area. How does this relate to behavior? A student who cannot keep up with class work may be left sitting, unable to participate. In the best of circumstances, boredom can ensue, and you know the saying about idle hands. The student who cannot keep up academically is also less likely to have access to positive adult attention from the teacher, and, as discussed previously, children will get attention from adults one way or another because they must.

Without access to positive attention that the other students receive by actively and successfully participating in the lesson, the student who is struggling academically may well begin to access teacher attention in a negative way. A dangerous downward spiral of undesirable classroom behavior, often accompanied by coercive attempts to stop this behavior, can be the undesirable outcome. A student unable to keep pace academically may also, in very subtle ways, become ostracized from other students in the classroom. If the teacher gives the struggling student a preponderance of negative feedback related to the content area of difficulty, other students may begin to view the struggling student in a negative way. This is particularly true for children in the younger grades.

The effect can be similar if, rather than giving attention comprised mostly of corrective feedback, the teacher gives a struggling student more negative attention than is given to the other students. If the classroom teacher is very diligent in not giving a struggling student a lot of negative attention and focuses on being positive with all children, the students may gravitate away from a struggling student all the same. Kids know who "gets it" and who doesn't. A struggling student is also likely to experience negative emotions—like embarrassment—if she feels that she is not as smart as the other students. Negative emotions can build upon themselves—in fact they tend *to* build on themselves—so embarrassment may ultimately become frustration and anger. In any event, these negative emotions are highly unlikely to make school feel like a safe, nurturing place to be or to promote a lifelong love of learning.

Such negative emotions are completely contrary to learning. If the struggling student feels isolated enough to eventually drop out of school, we know that statistically she has placed herself in a very high-risk category for additional, ongoing problems in life. If the struggling student gets ostracized from peers, statistically the odds are likewise against her experiencing positive outcomes. If exiled from a positive peer group, a student is much more likely to get in with the wrong crowd and begin a cycle of problematic behavior that can be difficult to change. This leads inexorably to Waller's Seventh Rule of Child Behavior Management: *In school, there is no wrong crowd, and don't create one.*

Consider Their Point of View

As adults, we have the ability—at least to some extent—to contextually avoid things that we find aversive. For example—if a family member calls us on the telephone—usually a family member who has a history of calling on the telephone when he wants to borrow some money—we can use caller ID to avoid answering these undesirable calls. We will do this because the family member in question wants to borrow money in the same sense that he would borrow a piece of chewing gum. Thanks to caller ID, we do not have to forego talking on the telephone to sincere and empathetic telemarketers just so that we can avoid someone who wants to unscrupulously talk us out of our money.

Children, however, have much less freedom to contextually avoid. Thus, the student doing badly in math—since his coming to school at all means that he is unlikely to be able to avoid math—may generalize his dislike of one academic subject to becoming a student who doesn't want to come to school for any reason, similarly to the way that Little Albert generalized his fear from white things to many white objects such as the beard of Santa Claus.

THE PROBLEM OF STUDENT DISENGAGEMENT

Many children today do not seem to be invested in the school environment. We, the adults and rulers of the world, express concern about what we perceive to be their lack of investment because we want our children to grow up and be functional enough to remain employed and contribute their payroll taxes, indirectly, to our social security retirement benefits. Adults, therefore, are likely to perceive children's lack of interest or success in school as a bigger problem than said children. It is often heard in popular media sources that our schools lag academically behind the educational programs in other parts of the world such that it is more reasonable to expect to receive accurately computed right angles from a (marching) penguin in Antarctica than from a high school student in your neighborhood.

Increasing the Difficulty of Unmet Standards

One of the primary ways that this perceived lack of smarts is being addressed is that federal and state educational mandates are putting in place much stricter curriculum requirements. More simply, the solution to the problem of assuming children are not invested or successful in schools is that the government mandate approached solving the problem by making school harder. This is the kind of reasoning that would lead you, if you were the manager of a baseball team, to solve the problem of addressing your best pitcher's poor performance tonight by gluing the fingers of his pitching hand to the toes of his left foot prior to his next game. Imposing more rigorous curriculum standards for students who may already be struggling is not the only corrective policy being implemented. We are also addressing the needs of students who are not invested in the school community and feel disconnected from school curriculum by providing them with fewer curricular choices. For example, some states have already done away with the vocational high school diploma track. In these places, students can choose any high school diploma track they want as long as it is the college preparatory track.

It certainly may be more challenging to maintain the interests of students who are understandably more concerned with mastering a video game involving the safety and welfare of a character whose very lives—all three of them—depend on his avoiding barrels being thrown at him by a large monkey than with getting students to maintain attention on school content that seems to have no purpose to them. However, children can become invested in pursuing and obtaining school success. A child's largest social network is made available to them by and, in essence, a child's job is going to school. She may gripe about school, but, if school is a safe and interesting place and if she were given a few days off, she would probably begin to ask to go back to school, if for no other reason than being able to fight the craving for those tasty cafeteria steak nuggets no longer. My youngest daughter, for example, recently received a peanut butter and jelly sandwich from her school cafeteria that was frozen. Think of the extra love and effort that went into providing a child with a frozen PB&J.

Academic skills deficits can be difficult to identify because children often try to mask such insufficiency to avoid negative attention and embarrassment. In contrast, a student in the school setting who has deficits in important social skills is often as immediately obvious as having surgery with a deficit of anesthesia. Any child is capable, under the right (or wrong) circumstances, of developing social skills deficits that can have a dramatic negative impact on the school experience. It is not an issue of character, genetics, or intelligence; it's a matter of learning.

There's Nothing Social About Social Skills Deficits

We can assume that Peanut, handsome rascal that he is, simply radiates social gravitas. However, any child can miss learning an important social skill, and you can't tell that a needed skill is absent by how a child looks. Once a needed social skill goes unlearned, it is easy for the unlearned social skill to negatively impact Peanut's social interaction and to begin even in small ways to limit his social environment. The more isolated he becomes, the more likely Peanut is to miss learning even more social skills, so much so that within weeks Peanut has become so socially ostracized that his only realistic vocational opportunity is hand modeling. Strangely—and this is one reason that social skills can be easily misinterpreted as willful problem causing—Peanut may be able to verbally tell you what the social skill involves, though he can still be unable to perform that skill in applied social situations.

Before you assume that I have recently consumed a beverage derived from certain varieties of mushrooms, consider the following. Has there ever been anyone in your social world who, though not particularly unlikeable, inspired in you a desire to avoid their company, similar to the way that the smell of dog food inspires you want to avoid eating it? This person maybe looked at the wrong place on your face when talking to you. Maybe this person blinked his eyes way too much. Maybe this person stood too close to you when talking. How could this person, an otherwise reasonably intelligent adult related to you only by marriage, arrive at the point of making you so uncomfortable and so strongly filling you with a desire to avoid him? A subtle dearth of social skills, that's why. Whatever the reason the social skills were not learned, the result is that among your most cherished longings is not to have to sit next to this person every stinking year at Thanksgiving, just like your students will avoid ostracized students at lunch or in group work and other situations.

Think about the social skills listed above that are so genetically deficient among your in-laws. How did you learn these skills? Did your mother tell you how frequently to blink your eyes when conversing with another person? Did your father walk around the mall with you, going up to people with a yardstick in his hand and teaching you how far to stand from someone you talk with (although, as the father of daughters, I may give this idea some more thought). These are social skills that we learned by interacting in social situations with others and from the model provided by others. Through the process of watching others and by trial-and-error practice, you learned to interact with people in a way that is not bizarre to them.

Looks Can Be Deceiving

Peanut is a bright, good-looking kid. There is no obvious reason that his social skills would not be at least as good as his peers. But assume for a moment that Peanut is just not a good visual learner. He didn't learn how far to stand from somebody he was talking with the same way that most other people in the world except your brother-in-law learned. He consistently stands too close to people. As a result, people may become inclined to avoid Peanut. Unfortunately, because most people learn many of their social skills from the models provided by other people and by trial-and-error practice and correction, being avoided by others results in Peanut acquiring fewer age-appropriate social skills, too. The process builds on itself, and Peanut becomes the kind of social pariah that invariably sits right behind you every time you go to the theater and has what sounds like a highly communicable coughing illness.

Even if you told Peanut to stand exactly 27 inches away from someone he is talking with, he is unlikely to pick up the skill just from receiving verbal instructions. Do you have a yardstick in your pocket? Do you know how far 27 inches from another person is? You can tell Peanut to stand 27 inches from someone he is talking with *every* day for a year, and there is still a good chance that Peanut will not be able to put the skill into real-world application without lots of real-world, applied practice and positive corrective feedback.

After extensive practicing of social skills involved in making conversation with you, and even after getting good at them with you, he may still fail miserably if he tries to engage in conversation with, say, a girl his age. Those two conversations are entirely different, so he may or may not generalize skills in having conversations with you to having a conversation with a peer. We do not need to strive for perfection in Peanut's social skills repertoire, such that he is likely to be invited to enjoy high tea with the ridiculously dressed royal sovereign of another country or maybe even a third runner-up from American Idol, but we do want Peanut to have functional social skills that promote successful peer interaction.

The outcomes of not possessing social skills that facilitate successful interaction with peers can vary, but the path often leads to behavior challenges. I have seen social skills deficits manifest in Peanut in a variety of ways. Unable to start conversations in a way that promotes peer interaction, he may resort to frequent name calling as a method of initiating social interaction. I have seen Peanut smack peers and laugh or smack and then run away giggling. I have seen Peanut grab purses and pencils and notebooks. These behaviors are often Peanut's attempts to engage his peers socially, and the attempts are successful at getting attention and responses. Unfortunately, these behaviors, getting the wrong kind of attention, create a larger social schism between Peanut and his peers as well as disrupting the classroom. I also have seen Peanut become completely unproductive in terms of academic output and begin to sleep through the school days. In fact, the most challenging students I have ever worked with have been adolescent males who were completely isolated from peers and who had responded by sleeping through the school day. These problems, though, can be caught early or circumnavigated completely. The most important thing to remember in striving for these goals is that social skills can be taught, taught, TAUGHT.

Knowing that skills deficits can be the starting point for behavior problems, you may have made the next logical inference: some target behaviors exist entirely because a student has skills deficits. If you, therefore, catch these target behaviors early and remediate skills deficits quickly, you will probably not need further intervention. Very recently I conducted training on function-based intervention planning for a group of school psychologists. During a break, one of them approached me and told me a story of a situation at her school that perfectly illustrates a very undesirable target behavior solely resulting from skills deficits. Prepare yourself mentally, physically, and spiritually, and I will share:

The Sordid Saga of the Mystery Pooper

As the first day of school came to a close, the administrative staff reflected on how things had gone. There were no major behavior problems, no major parent problems, and no major teacher problems. There had been a few minor disruptions, but nothing that exceeded the normally expected issues endemic to first days back at school. Not until, that is, the nightmare began.

This nightmare began where all school nightmares begin—in the principal's office. The principal had already labeled today a success and his mind had shifted away from school and to his evening. His reverie was shattered when a custodian burst into the office. The custodian's face told the whole story—follow me, we have big trouble. The principal followed the custodian into the bathroom and the custodian stopped in front of the last urinal in line. The custodian took one step sideways, and the principal saw. Saw and remembered. Someone had entered this room for the typical reason, but they had used the urinal for a purpose it was not designed. This grizzled veteran of educational leadership had two reactions: shock and awe.

After thinking about this event, surely the strangest he had ever seen outside of a parent teacher association meeting, the principal decided that this adulteration of school property was probably just a horrible prank to begin the school year with an event worthy of a yearbook write-up. Better to just let things pass quietly and move forward with the business that he was paid to tackle—keeping talking to a minimum in the lunchroom. Or so he thought until he was struck low by a dirty bomb the very next day. The elusive excrementitious errant had done it again.

The principal decided on a course of action. Wanting to tolerate no quarter, his course involved calling in the big guns. Thus, he circulated a memorandum carrying the full weight and power of the office from which it came. The decree was that teachers would periodically walk into the bathrooms and make sure that there was nothing heinous occurring. This show of force, surely the most intimidating the world has seen since the NATO Alliance, would serve the purpose of preventing such a disrespectful display from fouling his school again. Unfathomably, though, the fearsome might and terrible visage of a vigilant teaching staff did not serve as an effective deterrent. The fouling continued day after day without interruption. By Friday, the teachers were in a state of unrestrained terror, not knowing where or when the culprit would strike next. This state of unrestrained terror was probably unnecessary, however, since the crime, committed with the stealth of a coconut-scented tropical breeze, occurred in exactly the same bathroom and in exactly the same urinal every time. The faculty lounge was unlikely to be the next target of evil. By Friday the teachers had put a name on their nemesis. He was now known as the Mystery Pooper. And this same day one school administrator stood up and said no more to scatological tyranny. This man, already battle scarred from service with valor as the sergeant at arms of the Rotary Club, declared war on the Mystery Pooper.

There were casualties, to be sure. The custodian, after witnessing the conflict rage for two weeks, developed an acute stress reaction and was placed on workers compensation (actually, I made that part up because I thought it added personal tragedy and dramatic flair to the story). Rumors began to circulate that the fracas involved unconventional tactics for achieving the goal of winning. The board of education was approached for funding for DNA tests. The identity of the Mystery Pooper became more coveted than succulent pork loin. The Mystery Pooper was avowed by all to be a psychopathic miscreant with absolutely no appreciation for fine porcelain. One teacher told everyone that she thought she remembered reading somewhere that a child willing to so flagrantly violate a urinal was almost certain to grow up preferring cats over dogs and getting his underwear secondhand from Goodwill. This teacher was wrong.

A fog of battle fatigue and despair settled over the school. The principal's most fundamental article of faith and his personal slogan—"right always prevails and I am always right"—began to feel uncertain (the part about right always prevailing, of course, not the other part). But history, as it often happens, was subject to whim, accident, and serendipity. Just as the battle seemed unwinnable and surrender appeared to be the only solution to the stalemate, the secret alarm sounded in the east wing hall. The principal fled his office and ran toward the call. Entering the bathroom, he saw two teachers flanking the frequently fouled fountain, upon which sat a boy in the prekindergarten program. At the scene of the atrocities sat the Mystery Pooper.

The original records have been heavily redacted. The story has faded from civil memory, though it can be heard occasionally whispered in small unlit places by the shunned of society to younger siblings at bedtime. And history, fickle history, is written by the victors of a campaign, so we may never know all of the details of the story. We can tell you with certainty a few things. The Mystery Pooper was from the most rural section of a rural county. He was being raised by a single mother, as he had been since infancy. The two of them rarely left home such that the use of public restroom facilities was needed, and on these rare occasions, he went to the restroom with his mom. The Mystery Pooper was not a fledgling psychopath, nor did he have conduct disorder or oppositional defiant disorder. Heck, he didn't even have attention deficit hyperactivity disorder. He was just a boy who saw his first urinal on the day he started school. It hung lower on the wall than the other urinals, yet was slightly higher than the toilets. It was just right. And like Goldilocks before him, he took his respites where he was most comfortable.

This story relates directly to Waller's Eighth Rule of Child Behavior Management: *If there is a negative and a positive interpretation that can be made about her behavior, the child deserves and should always get the benefit of the doubt.*

TEACHING ALTERNATIVE BEHAVIOR

Academic and social skills deficits are not the end of teaching opportunities in behavior change. I do not remember who originally said it, but I once heard a quote that can be paraphrased as "behavioral science is like natural science in that nature abhors a vacuum." In the classroom, this suggests that any behavior intervention plan (BIP) that we develop is much more likely to be effective if we identify an alternate behavior that we teach to replace the target behavior.

Behavior that has been practiced repeatedly and over time becomes stereotyped or habitual. When you are initially learning to drive, driving takes a lot of your attention in order for you to do it well. With more practice, driving becomes a behavior so automatic that you can drive without thinking about it. In fact, on your way home from work, you may drive for miles and pull into your driveway and realize you remember almost nothing of the trip home. You were on autopilot; you have practiced so much that you can do it without thinking or while eating watermelon.

Once home, you start work on your newest home-improvement project based on a television show that suggests all sorts of improvement projects that it assures that you can do yourself because this television show does not know you. You are in the yard trying to attach two pieces of lumber together with nails, when, during a particularly mighty hammer swing, you strike your thumb instead of a nail. If you are anything like me, the hammer causes a signal to transmit along the nerves in your arm straight into a section of your brain that automatically causes your mouth to open and loudly say a bad word. You didn't plan to do this and make the neighbors look at you and wish that you would move to another town. But in times of stress and emotional arousal, our ability to think and problem solve is dramatically curtailed. We do not resort to a plan or something that we have previously been told because in times of stress we go with practiced behavior.

From an evolutionary standpoint, this has served an important purpose. When a saber-toothed tiger appeared before a distant ancestor, our ancestor didn't contemplate whether the tiger was hungry or not or whether, perhaps, this big cat was a vegetarian. Like yourself, your ancestor during such a time of peak stress went with stereotyped behavior by, like yourself, saying a bad word and then by running. Suppose a child in your classroom with a history of doing badly in math began saying bad words whenever it was time to do math. Saying bad words is extremely effective at getting someone out of math, so your student has been doing this a while.

Your punishing this student for saying a bad word is unlikely to change his behavior—even if you have remediated deficits in math. He learned that math is unpleasant, he has experienced failure and embarrassment during math, so being presented with math work causes an increase in his emotional arousal. In this state, during times of arousal when it is not the thinking part of the brain that is

Figure 2.1 Professional Educator Personality Matrix

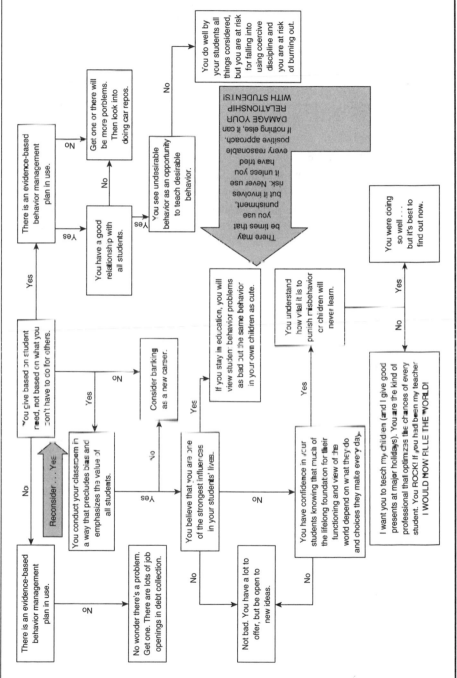

in charge, he will likely engage in stereotyped behavior. Further, trying to punish such behavior relies on the hope that the punishment will be even more unpleasant than math, which is not certain by any means. Part of a good BIP, therefore, involves identifying an alternative behavior and supervising the practice of the alternative over and over again until the alternative behavior becomes a habit.

Changing behavior is going to be a huge portion of your job. This will call on your strongest area of professional competence almost every time—your teaching ability. The rest of your intervention will be largely based on the way that you approach and assumptions you make about behavioral issues. Answer the questions in the Figure 2.1 decision tree and, if you are allowed to continue in the education field, move to the next chapter, where the ways to get started problem-solving for student undesirable behavior are discussed.

CHAPTER NOTES

Remediating academic or social skills is best approached by using evidence-based practices, or practices that have strong research support. The following Web sites provide such research-supported practices for academic and social skills areas:

National Dissemination Center for Children with Disabilities
http://research.nichcy.org/Evidence_TOC.asp

U.S. Department of Health and Human Services Substance Abuse & Mental Health Services Administration: National Registry of Evidence-based Programs and Practices
http://nrepp.samhsa.gov/index.htm

National Education Association
https://www.nea.org

CHAPTER THREE

Getting Started Through the Back Door

Indirect Assessment

A s is true for any type of assessment, some information is of better quality than other information. Nonetheless, even weak information can be extremely useful, especially if placed in the context of other information derived during your assessment. The first approach to data gathering when conducting a functional behavioral assessment (FBA) is often called indirect assessment. Indirect assessment is the least involved, least sophisticated approach to FBA. Indirect assessment involves collecting information indirectly or from indirect sources—hence the name. Indirect assessment includes looking at data that are largely already available to you in an attempt to develop a hypothesis about the function of a target behavior. You are developing a hypothesis because, when it gets right down to it, you don't know the function of a behavior. You are using all of the data you collect to make an educated guess. Indirect data can come from a variety of sources that already exist, such as the following:

- Bus reports
- Office referrals
- Homework completion
- Work samples

These sources of information are gathered indirectly, in that they are not the result of actually observing the target behavior of a student in a natural setting such as the classroom. The good news about indirect assessment is that this type of data collection and analysis is something that teachers already do. Doing this will not increase your workload, certainly not in a substantial way. The primary difference between the traditional approach to reviewing these data and our review for FBA is that you are thinking about all the information you collect through the lens of looking for clues and trends about the function of a target behavior.

For example, if Peanut is having behavior problems and your examination of work samples indicates that his work is below the level of performance typical of his classroom peers, this may be suggestive of academic skills deficits that are increasing the likelihood of the problem behavior occurring. Incidentally, if he finishes his work accurately and faster than his classmates and sits unengaged for stretches of time, this also suggests something about his challenging behavior—maybe he is bored. If you examine office referrals and see a pattern emerge wherein Peanut is getting in trouble around the same time of day or with the same teacher, this finding could be a useful clue that proves helpful in increasing the accuracy associated with hypothesizing the function of the behavioral issue—undesirable behavior might relate to specific school content or to specific people.

INTERVIEWS

The primary addition to your workload when doing indirect assessment will be interviews. Interviews are an integral part of a good FBA. Many school systems develop their own interviews that are sufficient and targeted to their needs and may be only two pages or so in length. When I conduct an FBA, I prefer to use an extensive interview called the functional assessment interview (FAI). The reason I prefer the FAI is that it is very thorough and focused on helping you formulate an accurate hypothesis about the function of a target behavior. It is many pages in length, but you, as an involved teacher who already works with the child, may know much of the information being sought before actually interviewing anyone.

I have sought the opinion of my students who have used both the more time-intensive FAI and abbreviated school-developed interviews. Their feedback consistently favors the FAI. Specific reasons that they have mentioned include the following: the interview is developed in such a way as to preclude forming negative opinions about a student, the length of the instrument prevents your obtaining information that is skewed because of bias, the extent of information obtained provides more insight about the student and their circumstances, and the FAI asks some questions more than once in a different format, which increases the odds of getting accurate data. Regardless of what interview you use, I will offer a few tips about doing them. These tips will not take the place of good training, good experience, or both, in how to go about interviewing others, but they are some lessons that I have learned that might also be helpful to you.

Interviews Are Potentially a Relationship Builder

Interviews provide an opportunity for substantial interaction between educators and caregivers. No parent or caregiver wants to receive word from a teacher (or anyone else, for that matter) that their child is having behavioral problems. However, I have found that people tend to be much more receptive to participating in problem solving with the school, just as surely as they tend to be put off by complaints about their child or by discussions around the theme of trying to identify "what is wrong" with their child. On many occasions when conducting an interview, I have needed to repeatedly reassure caregivers that I was not trying to find out what was wrong with their child or wasn't trying to diagnose their child before they were willing to talk with me in an open way. I usually will need to tell people repeatedly that the goal in asking these questions is to try to find factors associated with a problem behavior so that we can change the environment or circumstances and increase the odds of seeing the behaviors that we desire in the school setting.

It is not atypical for caregivers to have had numerous, unpleasant conversations with the school if their child has behavioral difficulties. Caregivers may have been asked to come to the school for meetings discussing their child's behavior. They may have received calls while they were at work, potentially causing trouble or embarrassment.

That the behavior problem is the fault of caregivers may be implied. Interviews can provide nonaccusatory, ample opportunity for not just getting information but also for normalizing behavioral issues with a problem-solving and collaborative approach.

Other teachers who are knowledgeable about Peanut and the target behavior can also be interviewed. Your colleagues might well provide additional invaluable insight. Does the behavior occur with all teachers? Does it occur throughout the school day or is it more localized to specific times of the day? Does it happen in classes such as art, music, or physical education, or does it happen only in academic classes? Interviewing colleagues also can be an educational opportunity. Not only might you learn information that promotes more accurately hypothesizing about the function of a problem behavior, but you can also use the opportunity to educate colleagues about the FBA process and team-build around the theme of problem solving.

When everyone involved understands that the purpose of an FBA is not to find someone to blame, the FBA process tends to be well accepted. Keep in mind, though, that as surely as interviews can be a relationship builder, they can destroy relationships if done badly or in a confrontational, accusatory manner. There is undoubtedly a time that you should offer your professional opinion in a direct way—but during an interview is probably not it.

Home Court Advantage

When I do an FBA as a school consultant, I always offer the caregiver the option of home court advantage for participating in an interview. In other words, I offer to come to their home at a time convenient for them. Obviously I don't invite myself into a home (unless I smell bread baking), but I do make the offer, and I also offer to meet them at their child's school if they prefer or feel safer. Particularly when a child has been having behavior problems at school, caregivers may have become defensive and unresponsive whenever they hear from school personnel. Giving caregivers the home court advantage tends to make them more comfortable, making it more likely that your discussion with them will result in getting useful information. I don't know for certain that there is a message in the following observation, but it is at least fascinating to me that only one caregiver has ever chosen to meet me at a school. The rest have chosen home court advantage.

Show Due Respect

It is always good to remember that no one knows a child better than her caregivers—so you want the caregivers on your team if even remotely possible. You may actually spend more time with a child during weekdays than caregivers do, but they still know the child better. Even if they don't, it is likely that they will nonetheless have information about their child that is useful to your doing an FBA and with problem solving. While you may not be in a position allowing you to go to someone's home, or you might not want to go even if you are in the position, there are still fundamental guidelines you can follow to team-build with and work collaboratively with caregivers:

- Face-to-face contact is better. If you can't meet face to face, accommodate the caregiver's schedule with a phone interview convenient to his or her schedule.
- Never allow communication about a problem behavior to be your first significant contact with parents. Make sure that you have given them previous positive feedback about their child. Start on day one.
- Don't use gunboat diplomacy. When caregivers interact with schools about a behavioral issue involving their child, it is often in a forum in which there are far more educators than caregivers. Don't outnumber the caregivers. If you must outnumber them numerically, don't outnumber them psychologically.

Keep No Secrets

When interviews are being done, the most common method is the interviewee is talking and the interviewer is sitting there and taking notes about what is being said, but the interviewee is never told what the interviewer is thinking and writing. Don't you hate it when you go see your physician, she writes notes in your record while glancing at you suspiciously over her clipboard, and you leave her office feeling vaguely uncomfortable and wondering if she has seen pictures of you on spring break? When I do interviews, I make LOTS of notes. When the interview is finished, I hand the notes to the person I was interviewing and ask her to review them and make sure I haven't made any mistakes or misrepresented anything she said. Invariably, the interviewee will stare at the notes like she was staring at a public toilet seat and refuse to touch them. I assure her that

I really want to make sure I have written down what she said accurately (which is absolutely true), and interviewees usually get into it. FBA does not lend itself to secrets.

Find the Setting Event if Possible

Interviews may provide your best chance of identifying the setting event of the target behavior. Setting events, sometimes called slow triggers, are factors occurring at an earlier point in the child's more distal part of the day or recent past that increase the likelihood that a target behavior will occur. They do not occur immediately before a target behavior—those are called antecedents (and sometimes called fast triggers).

Examples of setting events could include such things as Peanut coming to school without taking his medication (regardless of what the medication is), having a substitute teacher, or Peanut having a fight with his mother before he came to school. Any of these could make it more likely that Peanut will engage in challenging behavior at school, setting the stage for the target behavior to occur. Knowing the setting event can be valuable information, but identifying it can be difficult because setting events often occur before Peanut comes to school. Interviews can give you the opportunity to search for commonalities and patterns that could lead you to the setting event. Interviewing caregivers can be the best source for identifying these commonalities and they may, in fact, have a good idea about what the setting event might be (though they probably don't call it a setting event).

The More the Better

Generally speaking, the more people that you can talk to who have knowledge of and routinely see the child and the target behavior, the better. You never know where you might stumble on a gold nugget of information. However, don't go wild with interviews—they take time, and at some point, the benefits cease to outweigh the costs in time. Use common sense.

Stick to Function

As a mental health person, I can theoretically justify asking people all sorts of things and act as though I need for people to convey deep, personal secrets in order for me to be able to help them with their problems. Because the teacher is frequently the most important person in their child's life outside of home and family, you may find that caregivers are willing to tell you deep, personal secrets in the hope or belief that it will help you help their child. However, you don't need to know a family's deep personal secrets to develop an accurate hypothesis about the function of a child's problem behavior. Stick with looking for information directly related to the behavior in question. Don't be a voyeur.

What Was Tried Last Week?

On several occasions, I have been doing an indirect assessment, trying diligently to gather the information needed to ascertain the function of Peanut's problem behavior, to find the following:

- The problem behavior was seen by a previous teacher or in a previous school.
- A BIP was developed.
- The BIP worked.
- The BIP is not currently being used.

If something has been tried before and it worked, your job might already be done for you. If something has been tried before and it didn't work, knowing about it may provide useful clues about the function of the target behavior as well as potentially providing you with an intervention that you need not waste time trying.

Decaf Is for Sissies

You would probably know to look into possible physical explanations for the target behavior without my saying it. Many medical conditions can result in behavioral problems. In fact, many medications can have behavioral side effects. For example, a potential side effect of one popular prescription sleep aid is that you can take this medication and awaken eight hours later with absolutely no memory of the previous night, even if you did things after taking this medicine and before going to sleep. You might find this side effect troubling if you awoke in the downtown section of a large unfamiliar city wearing a Tarzan loin cloth, cradling a Malibu Barbie doll, and in possession of absolutely nothing else except fearful uncertainty. This side effect can have the ironic result of directly causing you to experience sleepless nights for years to come. It is not just prescription drugs that can affect behavior, however. I have learned to always get a sense for the amount of caffeine and over-the-counter medications that a child consumes. If Peanut is drinking more lattes than I am, there can be behavioral implications, especially if he comes to school without one.

Bed Knobs and Broomsticks

As is prudent, I try to get a sense for the things a child has in her bedroom. Many children today have cable television, stereo, video games, cell phones, and numerous other possessions in the room ostensibly slept in. It is not uncommon for a parent to think that their child is going to sleep at 10 p.m. each night, when in fact their child is going to bed at 10 p.m. each night—in the sense that the child did enter the bedroom—watches television for several hours, and goes to sleep around 4 a.m. This means that Peanut will probably not be at his charming best during multiplication drills.

Who Likes Mr. Peanut?

One of the most important questions you need to ask is, "Can you tell me the name of Peanut's best friend?" You need to know if the student has a social network, and you need to know this for the home and school settings. If a student has friends at school and has a problem behavior, are his friends other students who are doing okay in school or are they students who frequently get in trouble? We want to intervene quickly to make sure that he doesn't become socially exiled from students who are generally doing well at school. If he has friends who are doing well, this can be important for several reasons. For example, it can suggest that his problem behavior is a localized piece of his school behavioral repertoire and that he has numerous skills we can build upon; it can also provide us with information that can be helpful with intervention planning. If Peanut has no apparent friends at school but he has active social contacts at home, the target behavior may well be associated with situation-specific skills deficits, fear or dislike of school, or academic deficits. If he has no active social contacts in either setting, it suggests a more global problem perhaps associated with social skills deficits or a mental health issue. The implications for intervention can vary widely.

Talk to the Student?

A frequent question that is expressed by people who are learning to conduct FBA is whether or not they should include the student in their list of people to interview. I can come up with very few arguments against interviewing the child and not including her in the behavior intervention plan (BIP) process. Talking with the student can provide you with information that is probably unknown to other interviewees—such as who in the building is her favorite adult—that could both provide clues about the function of a target behavior and might highlight information that proves to be helpful in support planning. Moreover, if you develop and implement a BIP without including her, she will still figure out that something is going on—and her response to your trying to slip her this unannounced secret intervention may be the factor that results in the BIP failing. Incidentally, relating back to the point above, I have found that it is always valuable to ask Peanut who his friends are. If you can't find evidence that he has friends at all, and he thinks that he is the school's most cherished heart and presence—or if the opposite is true—this can have significant implications for intervention planning.

An inquiry that regularly follows the question concerning the wisdom of interviewing the student with challenging behavior is, "What if Peanut just answers our questions by giving answers that he thinks we want to hear?" My response is, "Who cares?" A student who is saying what they think you want to hear apparently values—at least to some extent—your opinion of him. Plus, it is good to know if he knows what you want to hear. This, too, is important information. However, sometimes people have trouble internalizing Waller's Ninth Rule of Child Behavior Management: *Anyone who truly devotes her life to trying to help meet the needs of other people, especially children, must be willing to run the risk of being taken advantage of without taking it personally.*

An example of a student interview developed by a school I have visited can be seen in Appendix A. And one final point: if you plan to observe the student in the classroom (if he isn't in your class) make sure you observe before interviewing the student. Otherwise, the impact of your being in the classroom will be more significant.

RAPID ASSESSMENT INSTRUMENTS

There are numerous rapid assessment instruments (RAIs) that are available to assist with FBA. RAIs are paper-and-pencil questionnaires that can be completed by adults with knowledge of the child and the target behavior, and when scored provide a hypothesized function. Two examples of RAIs are the Functional Analysis Screening Tool (FAST) and the Problem Behavior Questionnaire (PBQ). These instruments only take about five minutes to complete and are extremely simple to score (in about one minute). Including RAIs in your indirect assessment will not increase your workload in any substantial way. Even better, they give you another source of information that can be helpful in formulating a hypothesis about the function of a target behavior, especially if the results from RAIs are suggestive of the same function as other data you have reviewed. However, do not place your overwhelming confidence in RAIs used in conducting FBA. The ones looked at by researchers have limited reliability and validity, so never base your hypothesis exclusively on their results.

INDIRECT ASSESSMENT IN CONTEXT

As you can see, a lot of information can be obtained by doing a thorough indirect assessment (IA). So much, in fact, that after doing a thorough IA you should be in a position to formulate—at least tentatively—a hypothesis about the function of the problem behavior. IA methods should be part of every FBA that you do.

As a school consultant, I find that IAs are rarely sufficient for the FBAs that I do, though I have successfully based a few BIPs on FBA consisting entirely of indirect data on a few occasions. In these cases, the target behavior has been what is sometimes referred to as a *high-intensity/low-frequency* behavior. For example, I was asked to conduct an FBA with a first-grade student who was physically aggressive toward teachers (high intensity), but this behavior was only occurring about once per week (low frequency). I was willing, for the sake of dedication, to sit in that classroom as long as it took for me observe and collect direct data that would help find the function of the target behavior while simultaneously getting paid an hourly rate, but the school seemed reluctant. Using the results of an extremely thorough indirect assessment, it appeared that this student, who was on the autism spectrum,

- was periodically getting overstimulated after being in a large group setting for too long and was essentially shutting down, an outcome of which was his noncompliance with teacher instructions or even neglect in responding to her, which
- began an escalation in teacher directives and confrontation that exacerbated his sensory overload, and
- after a period of this unresponsiveness and noncompliance, the teacher was taking him by the hand to lead him to time-out, at which time
- he would attempt to pull away from the teacher and slap her hand.

This picture of the problem emerged only because the teachers I interviewed were very open, informative, and honest and because they had begun to document his episodes of aggressive behavior. If a student is having particularly difficult behavior challenges, the school often begins to document behavior occurrences. Sometimes when this is done, the resulting documentation about the student and behavior looks something like this:

8:45 a.m.   Called another student a name.

9:30 a.m.   Used profanity. Warned him.

10:15 a.m. Pushed another student for no reason at all. Written up, called office, became aggressive with assistant principal, had to be removed from classroom. Suspended.

If you read that and you could make no sense of it at all, your reading of it was similar to my reading. Such information is completely devoid of value in FBA. I can understand such an approach to narrative data recording. Teachers are busy and may not have time to elaborate on a behavioral occurrence when their primary goal is getting things back under control and moving on with their teaching. Sometimes people are reluctant to provide a detailed objective description of the behavioral occurrence from fear that someone will blame them for the problem. However, this type of information will not facilitate intervention planning, so it in no way serves the best interests of the student. And don't forget—assigning blame is not problem solving.

In contrast, the teachers who provided narrative data that resulted in the successful BIP described below were very detailed and expressive in communicating a vivid picture of each occurrence. They were confident in their competence (as they should have been), they wanted the student to do better, and their goal was clearly trying to document evidence that would be helpful to the child, not helpful in getting the child removed from their classroom. I don't

Figure 3.1   Indirect Assessment Process Path

You have identified a behavior problem.	Conduct interviews. Focus on function. Make sure that physical issues aren't the source of the problem.	Administer RAIs.
There is an evidence-based behavior management plan in place.	Look through work samples. Is there evidence of academic skills deficit?	Look through your data for patterns and commonalities.
You have given the target behavior a clear, countable, operational definition.	Conduct records review. Is this a new or ongoing problem? Has a previous intervention worked?	The data are consistent and you have formulated a hypothesis about the function of the behavior. You may be able to skip to BIP.
If you answered no to any of these, go back.	Begin FBA/Indirect Assessment.	Data are helpful, but you're not confident that you can formulate an accurate hypothesis OR you have the resources to get more data. Move to next chapter.

think that abbreviating their documentation information for the sake of self-protection even occurred to them.

The main parts of our BIP, which eliminated his aggression toward adults, was to incorporate scheduled sensory breaks into his school day and to avoid touching him when he was overstimulated and experiencing tactile defensiveness. Ironically, accurately determining the function of high-intensity/low-frequency behaviors can be much more challenging than developing an accurate hypothesis about the function of high-frequency behaviors, even if the target behavior is high intensity. This is because it can be easier to identify factors associated with a behavior when you can actually watch the behavior occur five times per hour than it is to determine the function of a behavior you see occurring only one or two times a week. In the case of the high-frequency behavior, you can directly observe the behavior occurring and factors associated with it enough to acquire useful information.

CHAPTER NOTES

The Functional Assessment Screening Tool (FAST) can be obtained from Dr. Brian Iwata at the University of Florida. The functional assessment interview is available in the following:

O'Neill, R. E., Horner, R. H., Albin, R. W., Sprague, J. R., Storey, K., & Newton, J. S. (1997). *Functional assessment and program development for problem behavior.* Boston: Brooks/Cole.

I am extremely grateful for the generosity of my friend Mr. George Banketas for his willingness to share his school-developed FBA and BIP materials in this and in subsequent chapters (see Appendix A).

CHAPTER FOUR

Descriptive Analysis

After completing an indirect assessment, it may be reasonable—based on the information you collected, the severity of the target behavior, and other relevant factors—to develop a hypothesis about the function of a target behavior and to develop a behavior intervention plan (BIP) based on that hypothesis. Your BIP may effectively address the behavior problem. Because indirect assessment in the grand scheme of functional behavioral assessment (FBA) represents weak data, you need to be aware that there is a good chance that your BIP will not work because you did not identify the actual function of the behavior. If this is the case, or any time you have the resources to do so, you need to move to the next level of sophistication in FBA methodology—direct observation. Although there are a couple of ways this can be done, the most common approach is what is called a descriptive analysis (DA), also referred to as an A(antecedent)-B(behavior)-C(consequences) investigation. For beginners, I think it is best to limit ourselves to discussing this most common method of DA, which is probably the easiest to conceptualize and which is useful for most classroom problem behaviors.

TIPS ON OBSERVING THE CLASSROOM

Before considering specific functions of problem behavior, it may be a good idea to consider some basic tips relating to classroom observation. The first point is extremely important: if the classroom you are observing is not your own, no matter how unobtrusive you try to be, your presence will be known and felt—even if you are as sneaky as a cat, even if you can traverse an entire shopping mall without completing a marketing survey. Several years ago, I was asked to observe a child in preschool and see if I could assist with intervention planning for some problem behaviors that were highly disruptive. Knowing that my presence in the classroom could change the child's behavior, I used my superior intellect to devise the following plan: rather than going in the classroom myself, I set up a video camera in back of the room before any students arrived, turned the camera on, and left the room. I put it in a back corner, and it was partially hidden by a cabinet. When the students came in from breakfast (and this is the kind of thing that you wish were made up but is not), this 4-year-old child that I had outsmarted—who didn't know that I was coming or that anything different was supposed to occur in the room—walked into the door, danced a pirouette, walked straight back to the video camera, and put the lens cap on it.

Similarly, your presence in someone else's classroom is likely to impact adult behavior as well as student behavior. You can't expect the activities you observe to necessarily represent typical behavior. There are a few things that you can do to lessen the influence of your being there. It is probably better to enter the classroom before students arrive or during a transition. Plan to stay for a while. Even if your attendance affects behavior, the result will tend to decrease with time. People will begin to forget you are there. If there is a computer in the room, I like to sit by it—maybe I'll be mistaken for a tech support geek. Make sure to go do your observation at the time, place, and the circumstances in which the target behavior is most likely to occur.

Do not glare at the specific child that you came to observe like they just took your turn at a four-way stop. Observe the whole class. Sometimes, I do not even initially ask teachers to identify the child I am supposed to be observing so that I can see if I can pinpoint her myself. Do not be obvious in your note-taking or data collection. I am frequently amazed at how quickly children figure out if you are counting something that they are doing. If a child looks at you, smile, but then break eye contact and look away. This will help prevent students from getting distracted from their lessons and help keep children from focusing on you—which will tend to change their behavior. Stay in the classroom through several activities because transition times can be notorious opportunities for behavior problems to occur.

Watch to see if there are classroom routines that the students seem to know and follow—and note any students who don't seem to follow these customs. Consider the availability of classroom rules— if you are observing a younger child, are the rules posted? Are the rules ever alluded to or discussed? Brainstorm a list of adjectives that you might use to describe the class, such as interesting, quiet, orderly, and democratic. How is participation sought or recognized? Are there disruptions from outside the classroom?

Consider your expectations as you observe. Do you know the student? Do you have a positive—or negative—opinion about her behavior? Typically, I will not review a student's records until after I have observed her at least once, because I want to minimize any bias I might develop from reading her description as written by others. Do you already know the classroom teacher? If so, do you consider her to be among the best in her profession or do you think her competence and skills would be better applied to work involving filling potholes and other road work? Do you generally have a positive or negative opinion of teachers? It is important to remember that the things that you expect to see can impact what you should have seen as well as influencing what you think you saw. See?

Watch the classroom dynamics. Is the lesson proceeding in a formal way, or are different activities occurring simultaneously. Is a quiet room rigorously maintained, or is some level of noise and activity acceptable. Are students given opportunities to respond, or are they primarily doing independent seat work? Where does the teacher typically position herself? Does she move around the room? Pick a few random students in the classroom as frames of reference to the student that you are observing. Compare whether all students get similar access to and responses from teachers and from peers. Finally, if you are observing someone else's classroom, make sure that, after your observation, you ask the teacher if the behavior you observed during your observation time was typical and representative or if it was markedly different than usual. If not typical, how was it different? Doing this will help you determine how much your presence may have had a bearing on student behavior. And keep in mind Waller's Tenth Rule of Child Behavior Management: *No matter how long you watch a kid, never forget that you can't see her world, only what she shows you of it.*

As you might guess, an A-B-C analysis involves identifying the (A)ntecedents occurring prior to the target (B)ehavior as well as the (C)onsequences that follow the target behavior. In my opinion, the most difficult part of doing an A-B-C analysis is being vigilant and open-minded enough to identify all plausible antecedents associated with a target behavior. You can begin to narrow the range of options after observing for a while, but initially you should have no preconceptions. For example, in one case of a child engaging in aggression toward adults and peers, the antecedent was finally identified as someone near the student coughing. There is no way to offer you a comprehensive list of antecedents, but consider the following common examples:

- Classroom directions
- Task demands
- Transitions
- Fire alarm
- Success
- Failure
- Teasing

Antecedents can be counterintuitive. Consider the exemplar of success. If a student attempts to act in accordance with instructions, your praise might be a reinforcer and she might try even harder in the future to comply with your directions if you give her praise for work attempted. If a student has experienced significant school failure or negative feedback in some other area of life, you might praise a student for doing her work (antecedent), but, as a result of her history of school failure or negative interaction with adults, the student runs out of the classroom crying. In this instance, your praise may have been punishing and it may have reduced the likelihood of her doing assigned work in the future. You need to be open to all potential antecedents, even the paradoxical ones (such as sometimes needing to teach a child to accept success).

Identifying consequences is easier. When identifying those phenomena that follow a target behavior, focus on the big four functions of behavior or on permutations of them. Consequences can also vary hugely in presentation, but, in the big picture, are they related to attention, escape, tangibles, or sensory stimulation? The answer is probably yes.

FORM OVER FUNCTION?

One question that I am frequently asked is, "What type of form should I use to do an A-B-C analysis?" My honest and consistent answer is that my preference is to use a cocktail napkin from the

Operational definition of the target behavior:

_____

_____

_____

Location of observation:

Time of observation:

Activity or subject area:

Antecedents	Target behavior	Consequences related to attention, escape, tangibles, sensory

Record your observation results in the above areas.

Blue Room at a Holiday Inn or some scrap paper salvaged from the waste basket, though not something that contains any material that has been previously masticated by another mammal. I realize that some people obsess a bit over things like forms, so I would suggest something like the above.

In any event, you might be more comfortable, especially until you get the hang of conducting a descriptive analysis, having a form in front of you that can serve as a visual prompt or reminder, as long as you remember Waller's Eleventh Rule of Child Behavior Management: *Any form or assessment tool, no matter how good, is still just paper, and a dyed tree product can never approximate the depth, character, and soul of a child.*

The form shown above is exactly the type of data collection sheets used in completing the following DA. Consider these suggestions and think about how they might apply to the case example as we are beginning the process of conceptualizing your own DA in your own classroom (see Figure 4.1).

Figure 4.1 Domain Prompts for Descriptive Analysis

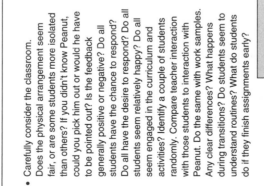

A-B-C

- You have a clearly defined target behavior. You have an array of potential antecedents, many of which are potentially listed in the previous boxes. When the target behavior occurs, what are the classroom conditions? What happens immediately after it? Does interaction from students or teachers change? Is there an attempt by the teacher to stop or redirect the behavior? Does the attempt occur the first time Peanut engages in the behavior or after he has done it a few times? Does it change if Peanut engages in the behavior several times? Does the target behavior have any effect on doing school work? If so, does the effect occur whether or not attention from others changes? Does the target behavior seem to occur regardless of what happens?

Social

- How often does the teacher interact and give feedback? Do teachers interact with Peanut similarly? Does Peanut attempt to interact with other students? How do they respond? Do students avoid or gravitate to Peanut? How do the students interact with one another? Does Peanut try to interact more when lessons are underway or during free time? Does Peanut's affect change when there are opportunities to interact with others? If so, how? How long does Peanut go between attempts to interact with others? Is Peanut more physically active than other students in general? Does his activity level change as he goes for longer times without interacting with others?

Classroom

- Carefully consider the classroom. Does the physical arrangement seem fair, or are some students more isolated than others? If you didn't know Peanut, could you pick him out or would he have to be pointed out? Is the feedback generally positive or negative? Do all students have the chance to respond? Do all have the desire to respond? Do all students seem relatively happy? Do all seem engaged in the curriculum and activities? Identify a couple of students randomly. Compare teacher interaction with those students to interaction with Peanut. Do the same with work samples. Any clear differences? What happens during transitions? Do students seem to understand routines? What do students do if they finish assignments early?

63

Case Example

An eighth-grade student identified as having an emotional/behavior disorder was engaging in out-of-seat behavior that was associated with disrupting other students when he was not on task. The student (Peanut, of course) also had a hearing impairment and was in possession of a hearing device, but he refused to wear the device in school. The target behavior identified was being out of his seat without permission during class. The definition of *out-of-seat behavior* was "a time period of more than five seconds during which there was no contact between the buttocks and the seating surface of the assigned chair during a lesson without first receiving verbal permission from the classroom teacher." *Permission* was defined as "raising one's hand and receiving verbal consent from the classroom teacher before getting out of his seat." An FBA was begun.

Indirect Assessment

Indirect assessment included record review, interviews, and completion of Rapid Assessment Instruments (RAIs). The Functional Analysis Screening Tool (FAST) and the Motivational Assessment Scale (MAS) were administered to adults with knowledge of the student and the target behavior. Interviews with involved adults familiar with the target behavior were conducted. The student was also interviewed, with particular interest given to ascertaining the kinds of things he enjoyed doing in his free time. The student said he enjoyed playing video games, playing computer games, and watching television.

A review of Peanut's records showed multiple disciplinary infractions for the current school year. He had served silent lunch 20 times, detention three times, been on Saturday work-detail once, and had received two direct office referrals. Both RAIs suggested the hypothesis that escape from undesirable academic tasks was the function of out-of-seat behavior. Interview data supported the same hypothesis, with interviewees consistently reporting a high correlation between increases in the target behavior and the student verbalizing statements such as "I hate this," or "When we doing something else?" No previously effective intervention was reported though numerous interventions (primarily the attempts to punish listed above) had been tried.

Descriptive Analysis

Table 4.1 is a sample of data from the DA:

Table 4.1   Classroom Observation Data Sheet

Operational definition of the target behavior: The definition of *out-of-seat behavior* was a time period of more than five seconds during which there was no contact between the buttocks and the seating surface of the assigned chair during a lesson without first receiving verbal permission from the classroom teacher. *Permission* was defined as raising one's hand and receiving verbal consent from the classroom teacher before getting out of his seat.

Location of observation: Ms. Smith's classroom

Time of observation: 11:15 a.m.–12:15 p.m.

Activity or subject area: Math/fractions, current grade average for reporting period: 67

Antecedents	Target behavior	Consequences related to attention, escape, tangibles, sensory
Bell ring, student movement, peer interaction.	Out-of-seat, doesn't meet definition standards because no lesson has begun.	N/A—class settling in time. All students in assigned seats within three minutes.
Conversation between two nearby students, teacher instructs, "Take out your books."	Out-of-seat, duration 2½ minutes, then returns to seat.	Peanut discussing contents of trash can, all other students have book on desk turned to assigned page within 30 seconds.
Peanut pushes paper off of desk, makes quiet mumbling noises.	Out-of-seat, Peanut frequently talking while walking around room, affect suggestive of affective arousal, duration two minutes, then returns to seat.	One peer watches Peanut, all others on task. Peanut has completed no work.
Teacher, moving around room offering individual assistance moves closer to Peanut, gives a quiet prompt to begin work.	Out-of-seat, Peanut goes to pencil sharpener, sharpens approximately two inches from pencil while humming.	Avoids teacher attention, no work attempted.
Peanut picks book up from floor, turns to assigned page, spins book in circles on desk.	Duration five minutes. Peanut walks to bookcase and scans book titles.	Teacher prompts him to return to his seat, he immediately complies. Materials now on desk, no work started.

We have now reached the most controversial part of DA—interpreting the data. You don't have the advantage of seeing all DA data, but what, if any, conclusions might you derive from the information above. Some of the movement and noises Peanut engaged in might intimate a sensory issue. You might be leaning toward attention as the function and assume that his out-of-seat behavior would worsen until Peanut received adult attention (although there is one suggestion that peer attention—the student watching him walk around—could be the function).

As with any data analysis, resist the urge to fixate on details to the exclusion of the whole. Consider the whole picture that Peanut's data paints for us. We have extremely consistent indirect data, all of which suggest that escape is the function of his out-of-seat behavior. We have multiple reports of his verbalizing how much he dislikes certain content. We know that he is not passing the subject area. We know that frequently the attempts to punish Peanut's behavior resulted in escaping.

Think about the observational data. Though it is far from conclusive, what, if any, patterns emerge? We see no immediate peer relation problems. Though accessing teacher attention is a potential candidate, we do not see any behavioral evidence (like frequent covert glances) that he has a strong—or stronger than average—need for adult attention. In fact, he actively avoided teacher attention. We saw no problems at all prior to the instruction to get out work materials, even though transitions are notoriously high-risk times when behavior challenges might occur. We observe several things indicative of a negative affective response, almost all of them directed toward content-specific stimuli. The only exception is his leaving the area to avoid teacher attention, which could instead be a desire to avoid the embarrassment of not knowing how to do the work. Finally, when he receives adult attention in the form of a prompt to return to his seat, he immediately complies with no argument. Arguing with directions is a superb way to maximize getting adult attention. The preponderance of evidence seems to insinuate a function of escape, specifically from undesirable academic tasks. Academic skills deficits may be associated with the target behavior.

Source: Brooke Khodabakhsh.

After you have completed DA, sit down with all of your data. Consider the results from indirect assessment (IA) and from DA. What does the evidence suggest? Is there clear support for hypothesizing a function of the target behavior? If you have conducted both IA and DA and have no direction for developing your hypothesis, it might be a good idea to call in assistance. If you have a good direction, you have a decision to make: Do you now skip to intervention planning or do you want the strongest evidence that you can get that you are on target with your hypothesis? If you want the strongest evidence that you can get, it's time to move to functional analysis.

CHAPTER FIVE

Functional Analysis

Functional analysis (FA) is the most sophisticated (i.e., difficult) form of functional behavioral assessment (FBA). FA is an FBA technique (though it is not unusual to hear the terms "functional analysis" and "functional behavioral assessment" used interchangeably [and incorrectly]) in which you experimentally manipulate the variables that you have hypothesized serve as the function(s) of the target behavior. If that explanation is a bit confusing, you can feel comfortable that you are normal and may be able to maintain relationships with people who do not require close supervision. I believe that an example will clarify any confusion that you may have better than the definition can.

In the following case, a boy was engaging in a high rate of talking out in the classroom, such that he was having both academic and social problems as a result. The classroom teacher labeled this target behavior as "irresponsible talking" and operationally defined the target behavior as *verbalizations not related to the current academic content made loudly enough to be heard by others and occurring without verbal permission during classroom instruction.* Because the previous example covered indirect assessment (IA) and descriptive analysis (DA), this case will not repeat those methods again in detail. It will cover how an FA can be done in the classroom setting.

The teacher did both IA and DA, and from the data developed the hypothesis that the function of the target behavior was (acquiring adult) attention and escape (from undesirable academic tasks). Before a behavior intervention plan (BIP) was put in place, however, the teacher wanted to be as confident as possible that her hypothesis was correct, because she hoped that colleagues would also use the

Figure 5.1   Irresponsible Talking

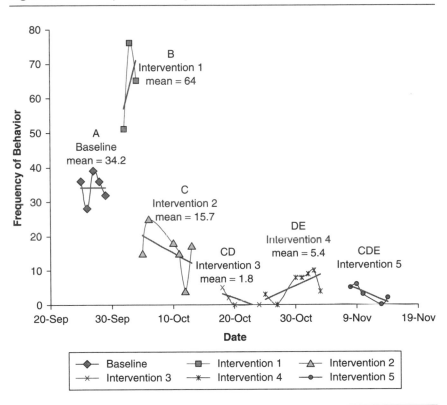

Source: Jenny H. Glenn and Raymond J. Waller.

intervention if it was found to be effective. After collecting baseline data (phase A), she found that Peanut was engaging in about 34 talk-outs per class period (see Figure 5.1). The goal of FA was to test her hypothesis, which was that her attention was a primary function maintaining the problem behavior.

If you thought that your attention was serving as the function of a student talking out, how would you test that hypothesis? That's right—in phase B, her *functional analysis*, in order to test her hypothesis that acquiring teacher attention was a primary factor in the target behavior, each time Peanut called out, she said, "Please raise your hand before you speak." She did this every single time that Peanut talked out in class, and note that she said it after the target behavior occurred. The reason for this is that if her attention was reinforcing irresponsible talking, the target behavior would increase when more attention was given. You can see in phase B that talking out nearly doubled during FA. Her hypothesis, that acquiring adult attention was a function of irresponsible talking certainly seemed supported by these data.

Teachers often make similar kinds of statements as a reminder and mild reprimand for minor classroom behavior problems (not realizing that this simple strategy, so easy to use without even thinking about) that, depending on the function of a target behavior, things could be made worse. People commonly refer to these attempts to mildly reprimand as "prompting" a student. These are not actually prompts. A prompt occurs before a target behavior. What is the difference? The difference is that such statements after a target behavior can reinforce the target behavior. Counterintuitively to conventional thinking, the statement that the teacher made—the goal of which was decreasing calling out—actually increased calling out. This is the logic of FA—to systematically test your hypothesis about why a behavior is occurring.

Why bother with this? Because, as in the example above, the FA provided strong evidence that the teacher was on target in hypothesizing that her attention was a factor in the occurrence of talking out. With strong evidence that you know why a behavior is occurring, you are armed with an excellent chance of effectively changing the behavior, because, and you may have heard this before, the intervention will be focused on the function of the behavior rather than the outcome of simply pulling an intervention out of the clear blue sky. And this teacher wanted to be as sure as she could because she wanted the cooperation of Peanut's other teachers. Nothing erodes collegial cooperation like being convinced to try an intervention that FAILS.

Her first intervention, designed to address the function of getting adult attention, was teacher-prompted self-monitoring. During IA she interviewed Peanut, who agreed his talking out was causing him trouble in most of his classes and further indicated that he would like to work with her to change that behavior. The teacher began giving verbal praise (her attention) for raising his hand rather than calling out. The effect of this was to no longer reinforce irresponsible talking after the talking had occurred but to provide him with a prompt (her attention) before the target behavior happened. Again, we are intervening by addressing antecedent conditions. You can see that this intervention (phase C) reduced irresponsible talking to less than half of the baseline (or original) rate. This was quite an improvement, but we thought we could do better.

You may recall that our IA and DA suggested that he engaged in irresponsible talking for adult attention and to escape from aversive academic tasks. Therefore, the next intervention that was introduced was targeted to address the function of escape. Once again, information gathered during IA provided evidence that his escape from academic tasks was strongly associated with the target behavior. In phase CD, the teacher began giving all of her students prompt cards with questions about the day's content that she might ask them aloud in class. On Peanut's card, however, she wrote both a question and the answer to that question. This provided Peanut a means to participate appropriately in class (as well as a way to continue to practice raising his hand and getting called on before talking). As you will notice, this combination reduced Peanut's talking out to zero, effectively resulting in Peanut being the least likely student in class to talk out.

In the world of behavior management, our job is to work ourselves out of a job. We want every student to demonstrate the behaviors that foster learning and positive social interaction with peers without the need of our intervention. Thus, one of the goals for which we strive is for all students to manage their own behavior. The next intervention (DE) reflects an attempt to move Peanut from teacher-prompted (which provided him with adult attention) self-monitoring to true self-monitoring (drastically reducing his access to adult attention), while the prompt cards were continued (addressing escape from undesirable tasks). The goal of moving to true self-monitoring was implemented too quickly, however, and the talk-outs began to increase again. Seeing this, the teacher quickly went *back* to prompting (giving Peanut her attention before the target behavior occurred), beginning to slowly incorporate components of true self-monitoring, and continued with academic prompt cards. The irresponsible talk returned to zero, and this rate was maintained throughout the school year.

You might reasonably pose the question at this point, "What was the advantage of giving Peanut the answers? Anybody could participate if given the answers." In this, of course, you answered your own question. Peanut was a young man who *never* participated in class in a desirable way. *Everything* that he did was reportedly disruptive and unpleasant to teachers. Since the beginning of the school year, he had not raised his hand to answer a single question! This intervention provided the opportunity to engage in behavior momentum. Remember earlier when it was said that negative emotions and behaviors tend to beget even more negative emotion and behavior? Likewise, the opposite is true—positive emotion and behavior beget more positive emotion and behavior. This is behavior momentum.

CHAPTER SIX

Multiple Functions

As seen in the previous case example, it is quite possible to have a target behavior maintained by more than one function. It is not hard to conceptualize how this becomes so and, in fact, is almost assured to become an issue if an undesirable behavior continues for a period of time. A student engages in a behavior that is not conducive to the school environment, and we intervene. The common strategies that we use, essentially ideas that we pulled from the air, will work for some children and adolescents but may have the opposite of the desired effect for others. Consider the previous example of Peanut's irresponsible talking. During the functional analysis, the teacher attempted to reduce irresponsible talking in class by giving a mild reprimand, instructing him to raise his hand before speaking, and the result was that his talking out became dramatically worse. She used an intervention that almost all teachers would try, but her intervention met his need for attention, reinforced the undesirable behavior, and his talk outs increased instead of decreased.

Now imagine that Peanut has an extensive history of irresponsible talking in school. This thought experiment may be easier for you if I tell you that, in fact, Peanut *had* an extensive history of the target behavior. He may have begun talking out because it provided a mechanism by which his need for acquiring adult attention was met (or, stated differently, teacher attention reinforced talking out).

However, as he talked out more and more, it began to get him out of math class because he was sent to sit in the hall or to time out or to the principal's office—and he had been having trouble with math. So not only was he getting the adult attention he needed after talking out, talking out started getting him out of undesirable class work. He was sent to the corner. He was sent to time out. He was placed in the hall. He was sent to the office. He was even sent to the counselor. In most of these situations, he received a lot of adult attention (which, don't forget, was the primary function of undesirable behavior). Not just adult attention, but intense one-on-one attention from an adult. He reveled in one-on-one time with the principal and the counselor.

Even though the goal of his being sent out of the classroom was to reduce a target behavior, the behavior strategies that many teachers would automatically try actually made things worse. The custodian would ask him why he was in trouble when he was sitting in the hall. Peanut received attention in some of these situations, *but* he didn't do math in any of them. Serendipity and happy days! He elevates the technique of talking out in class to a level of perfect performance usually associated with a spiritual calling.

Consider the traditional course for addressing disruptive behavior in schools. A student who does not respond to the common, minimal behavior-management strategies used in many schools begins a slow trek involving behavior escalation and more aversive interventions. These intervention strategies, often unrelated to the function of the disruptive behavior, were ineffective. They may have been aversive, but they were not punishing. After weeks or months of failed efforts, some of which made the target behaviors worse, a student support team (SST) convened to develop an intervention plan. The SST plan was basically to do more of the same things that were already not working. When this also astoundingly failed, evaluation for eligibility to receive special education services was begun. By this time, the undesirable behavior had occurred for a long time and had become useful for more needs than one.

However, the longer a behavior problem has persisted, the harder it tends to be to change. One reason is that it has been practiced longer, and practice makes perfect. Another reason is that a student who regularly gets in trouble at school is likely to become ostracized by peers or for his interaction with peers to become unpleasant (e.g., teasing, bullying, and so on). As separation from peers occurs and positive attention from them declines, Peanut becomes more dependent on adult attention (because we all need attention and will get it somewhere), which is the function of his undesirable behavior.

But the longer a student engages in problematic behavior, the more this behavior becomes associated with various functions—maybe adding a function of escape from unpleasant interaction with classmates or from unpleasant class work. It is in everyone's best interests to intervene early and intervene effectively with childhood behavior problems, which sometimes requires you to consider Waller's Twelfth Rule of Child Behavior Management: *Thinking that a child needs to be in someone else's classroom is much less likely to help him than your making a commitment to giving him your very best right here and right now.*

CHAPTER SEVEN

When to Use What

S o when you have a student with a classroom behavioral challenge, which of the described methods of conducting a functional behavioral assessment (FBA) do you use? I'm not certain that there is consensus on this. I will offer you my thoughts, based on my understanding of the research guiding FBA, personal experience in the schools, and the feedback of hundreds of my graduate students and practicing teachers. I caution you that these are my suggestions, and there are undoubtedly many—possibly billions—of researchers, educators, and practitioners who have their own (maybe different) opinions.

The first assumption that I make is that you already have an effective behavior management plan in place. A lot of teachers think that they have an effective plan in effect if students who violate their rules must move a clip based on a "three-strikes-you're-out" philosophy. You are not using an effective behavior management plan if a student, after breaking a rule, must have her license punched, or if nefarious rule-breaking students are sent to time out or to the principal's office. These are not effective behavior management approaches. They are more of a desperate hopeful guess than an effective behavior strategy.

If you are using a system like this, and it seems to be working for you, drop this book right now, scurry to the nearest convenience-type store, and purchase a lottery ticket. Your life is characterized by an amount of luck equal to or greater than the amount of luck involved in being a UPS driver whose favorite color is compost brown.

If you do not become independently wealthy by playing some government-sponsored game of (no) chance, and you are thus required to continue to earn your wages by teaching school, I need to tell you something: Peanut is coming. He may not appear today, he may not even appear next year, but I tell you that as surely as several nice people will be eaten by something in a Stephen King novel, if you teach long enough—Peanut is coming. And Peanut don't move no stinking clip. Peanut does need to be taught new skills and behaviors. He does not need to be feared.

With your effective behavior management plan in place, I suggest that any time you have a student who is breaking rules consistently *despite your behavior plan* that you should start an FBA. Likewise for the student who engages in an ongoing recognizable pattern of behavior infractions, regardless how minor. I say this for several reasons. First, to quote the greatest law enforcement officer in a generation—Barney Fife—"Nip it in the bud." As discussed previously, it is far preferable to go ahead and take the time to intervene early in the life cycle of a challenging classroom behavior while it is young and fresh than to try to intervene after it has been around for a while getting hard and grisly like your last attempt to prepare blackened fish.

Second, you will begin a data collection process that can be useful to others, should others need to become involved. Schools sometimes collect data like Yogi Bear collected picnic baskets—anywhere, anytime, they all are good, the more the better. However, if you are unsuccessful in changing behavior in the direction you desire, Yogi-style data collection will be completely useless to other people who are in a position to help you. That being the case, they will have to start over with their own data collection process, wasting valuable time.

Beginning the FBA while the behavioral concern is still minor will involve caregivers before your interaction with them relates to a crisis, meaning that you can take advantage of some of the relationship-building components of early stages of FBA. Finally, you will be approaching behavioral challenges in a helpful manner; unlikely to result in (or worsen) any stigma or labeling concerns that could arise.

So What to Do When, Already?!?

Any time you do an FBA, you should do indirect assessment. As mentioned earlier, your job as a teacher means that you will already be collecting much of this information. The FBA process will provide a focus and efficiency that might not otherwise exist. Components of indirect assessment can be relationship builders with caregivers, and it is always an advantage to have consistency in a positive and meaningful manner between home and school. Sometimes we like to place blame for student behavior problems on caregivers, though this is unlikely to be helpful, but, in my experience, the vast majority of caregivers have their child's best interests at heart. Do not neglect to admit that caregivers may place blame for their child's behavioral problems on *us* and disapprove of our methods and think we are to blame. In either scenario, the student is not helped.

Should you stop with indirect assessment? Again, you could find different opinions, but most would say no. The first consideration is this: if the behavior problem you are addressing is a danger to *anyone* in the classroom, or is so disruptive that you are unable to provide instruction for other students, this is a crisis situation. You do not have time to do an FBA of any type. You need to get immediate support from administration. These conditions cannot be allowed to exist in a classroom. If you are alone in the classroom and the behavior problem you are addressing is not a danger to anyone and is not so disruptive that you are unable to provide instruction, AND if the indirect assessment provides you with enough evidence to develop a reasonable hypothesis about the function of the problem behavior, then you can work from the evidence provided from indirect methods. This is especially true if you have more than one source of data that supports the same hypothesis about the function of the target behavior (e.g., results from your interview and from the Functional Analysis Screening Tool support the hypothesis that getting peer attention serves as the function of the challenging behavior).

The FBA up to this point may well have (1) fostered a good home-school working relationship and (2) provided data that allow you to accurately identify the function of a problem behavior. Even if your FBA *did not* facilitate the development of an effective intervention plan, then you have begun (1) a data collection process that will provide useful information to any subsequent support that you receive in changing the challenging behavior while (2) identifying an intervention that other people need not bother with though you have still been (3) relationship building with caregivers. Every possibility in these scenarios is positive. As previously discussed, I have done FBAs consisting of only information from indirect methods a couple of times from which a successful intervention plan was developed, but working from indirect data is far from optimal.

DESCRIPTIVE ANALYSIS

Whenever reasonable, descriptive analysis involving observation of the student including an antecedent-behavior-consequence (A-B-C) analysis in the natural environment is the minimal practice standard most practitioners strive for and that researchers advocate. No matter how much indirect data you have gathered, it is all, well, indirect. There is no good substitute for observation, and descriptive analysis will provide you with data giving you much more confidence in formulating an accurate hypothesis regarding the function of a problem behavior. Doing an FBA without including observation of the student is sort of like running a truck stop without knowing how to pump diesel. It's theoretically possible, but lacking the elementary hands-on experience puts you at a distinct practical disadvantage.

There are, however, a couple of logistical difficulties associated with conducting a descriptive analysis. If you are alone in your own classroom, it is virtually impossible to do one, or to do a really good one, particularly until you get some experience in FBA. It is extremely difficult to observe a student in your class objectively *while* trying to teach academic content *while* trying to identify every eventuality (including yourself) that might be the antecedent of a challenging behavior *while* trying to keep an accurate count of the target behavior. There is no way that you can do an FBA that meets scientific standards of acceptability by yourself. Fortunately, you get invited to parties and so are obviously not living in the scientists' world. You live in a practical world with social activities and a hobby. You may conduct descriptive analysis alone and, though very weak, the data may provide the practical information needed to effectively support plan.

Remember, probably the biggest difficulty associated with conducting a descriptive analysis is that it sounds so deceptively simple. You have a problem behavior—let's christen it "calling out." That is "b." All that you have to do is watch for Peanut to call out, note everything that happens before he calls out ("a," the antecedents) and everything that happens after he calls out ("c," the consequences). Oh, and you are to do this also while trying to teach.

Remember too, that another challenge of this procedure is that you have to consider every possible antecedent. The true antecedent to Peanut's calling out could be a huge variety of things: the light level, the noise level, the assignment, gastrointestinal distress, receiving verbal instructions, smelling your breath, receiving verbal instructions in a particular fashion or in the presence of particular people, the time, or the subject being taught. This list could go on as long as a regressive tax law, and there could still be antecedents you missed if you weren't watching carefully for all possibilities. The only way to begin to rule out possibilities is to observe the behavior long enough to see that those possibilities are not regularly associated with the problem behavior—and you're going to do this while you teach spelling? Actually, you can. Your work may not be published in a major scientific journal, but it very well may result in an effective behavior support plan.

When identifying consequences that follow Peanut's calling out, focus on permutations of the four common functions associated with school-based target behavior. A faint warmth may threaten to erupt into a blaze of understanding, kindling a small part of your brain that you rarely use   perhaps the part of your brain that knows that you do not really have any recently deceased relatives on another continent who left you a vast monetary estate overseen by legal counsel so dedicated to fulfilling your departed relatives' wishes to shower you with unearned money that these paragons of legal virtue will manage to track you down entirely by e-mail—allowing you to see that, with sufficient observation of the target behavior, a pattern of consequences will invariably emerge and be suggestive of the function.

After you have conducted the descriptive analysis, the ideal outcome is for you to have identified with a good degree of confidence the antecedents and the consequences that are associated with Peanut's calling out. If a pattern emerges, you are in a good position to develop a hypothesis about the function of Peanut's calling out. In fact, you will then have good evidence that should facilitate your formulating a good hypothesis—even more so if your observational data correspond well with your indirect data. There is a good likelihood that your hypothesis about the function of Peanut's calling out will directly facilitate the development of a successful intervention plan.

FUNCTIONAL ANALYSIS

Having collected both indirect and observational data, especially if they suggest a similar hypothesized function of Peanut's calling out, you are well positioned to have confidence that you are on solid ground with behavior intervention plan (BIP) development. You do not yet, however, have the strongest evidence that can be gathered and applied to the task of developing a hypothesis about Peanut's calling out. If you want the strongest evidence accessible through the FBA process, you must progress to conducting a functional analysis (FA). When you do an FA, you actually test your hypothesis about the function of Peanut's calling out. FA is not for the weak of heart. If your hypothesis about the function of a target behavior is that Peanut calls out for the purpose of acquiring adult attention (even if he receives negative attention), then an FA of this hypothesis would involve making his calling out *worse.*

Yes, worse. Simply stated, the way that you would implement an FA is to provide Peanut with reinforcement in the form of adult attention (even if it is negative attention) each and every time that Peanut calls out. If you are correct in your hypothesis concerning the function of his calling out—if adult attention is reinforcing this behavior—then his calling out will increase.

FOREWARNED IS FOREARMED

Is there a place, no matter how remote, in an orderly universe for conducting an FA? It depends. If you test the hypothesis that the function of calling out is acquiring adult attention and the calling out increases when you test this hypothesis, you now have a very high degree of confidence that it is, in fact, adult attention reinforcing Peanut's calling out behavior. You can therefore develop and implement a BIP involving the altering of circumstances under which Peanut receives adult attention and you can do so with a very high degree of confidence that your intervention will reduce or eliminate the calling out.

I offer the following thoughts on conducting a functional analysis. These are my guidelines (though you can probably find others who agree) and are not intended to establish policy or practice for your classroom or school or for the professional community. These are the guidelines that I extend to my graduate students in their own classrooms. First, if the target behavior is dangerous in any way or so disruptive to instructional delivery that student learning is impaired, don't do an FA.

If you do not have somebody from outside the classroom providing you support and assistance, don't do an FA. If the student with the problem behavior has any chance of going into another setting, like into someone else's classroom or into the cafeteria and getting into trouble in that setting because you increased the problem behavior and Peanut hasn't settled down yet, don't do an FA. It's not fair to cause trouble for a student, no matter how good the reason may seem. Finally, if the behavior of concern isn't something like calling out but involves either illegal or aggressive behavior, don't do an FA.

This last point could well be—and be well—argued by other people who do FBAs, especially as it applies to aggression, so I will give an explanation of why I believe what I do. My belief is based on a combination of research, experience, and extrapolation from related research findings and is not presumed to be suggestive of standard of practice in all educational settings. Some things that could be called "aggression" are developmentally appropriate. Even things that you might call aggression could be appropriate (in the sense that people receive money to do them) when done by adults who are wearing swim trunks and locked in a Texas cage match, have monikers like Granite Mandibles and BoBo Smasher, and can only be seen on pay-per-view until they get their big break and acquire a starring role in a children's movie.

It is not necessarily abnormal for younger children to push other children or to take a toy from another child without asking. Children tend to learn, as a result of teaching and exposure to cultural norms and expectations, not to be physically aggressive with other people. In fact, most children incorporate this expectation into their identity so thoroughly that many of them will not attempt to hurt another person unless they perceive a significant threat, are under extreme duress, or receive instruction to do so. I believe that for most children to physically aggress against adults is even more of a social taboo, learned earlier and adhered to more stringently than the taboo of aggressing against other children.

I also believe, however, that aggressive behaviors become easier once the line is crossed and such acts are committed, and that they become easier still the more times they are committed. In fact, once violated, the norms against violent or aggressive behavior can be hard to reestablish. In most cases therefore, it is my opinion that the negative impact of violating societal norms against aggressive behaviors, even to do FA, can be so consequential that the benefit of doing an FA is not worth the risk. As a result of these concerns, I refrain from doing an FA in almost all instances of aggressive behavior.

CHAPTER EIGHT

Summarizing and Reporting the Data

As a school consultant, after I have completed a functional behavioral analysis (FBA), I write a very extensive report that summarizes my interpretation of what the information means. This report is typically many pages in length. You have probably heard the old saying, "The data speaks for itself." That saying, like the title of most country music songs, is incorrect. No data speaks for itself! There must always be somebody to interpret and summarize the data collected. If you are conducting an FBA in your classroom, or even if you are part of a collaborative team of educators who participated in doing an FBA, you will probably want to summarize your data with some brief narrative write-up.

A narrative write-up can serve as a reference to which people can return as needed, it can serve as a record for future teachers, and it might serve as a component of progress monitoring of the behavior of a student. An example of a school-developed summary report can be found in Appendix B. There is a very good chance that your write-up can be much less involved and much briefer than mine, but it is still a good idea to summarize your information and include data-based recommendations for behavior intervention planning with at least a summary similar to Appendix B.

As you have seen from previous chapters, FBAs can range from simple data collection procedures to fairly complicated endeavors. As a result, I always provide a description of the assessment methodology that I used to accomplish an FBA. This prevents anyone who may at some point review the narrative summary from assuming that the data collected during the FBA were any stronger (or weaker) than they actually were. Because the FBA process can provide data that can range from weak to very strong, you may make intervention recommendations that also range from weak to very strong. I think that it is important to distinguish between recommendations made from weak data and recommendations made from very strong data for several reasons.

First among these is that, if you make recommendations about intervention planning that are based on very weak data, there is a higher probability that the intervention plan developed from the data will not work because you formulated an incorrect hypothesis regarding the function of the problem behavior. If you participate in developing a behavior intervention plan (BIP) that will be used by other people and if the BIP does not work, the people who tried to implement the ineffective BIP may become disenchanted with the FBA and the function-based BIP process, and thus be tempted to resort to traditional and potentially harmful discipline strategies. Such a response would be counterproductive because FBA and function-based BIP are the strongest, most empirically supported approaches available for changing challenging classroom behavior problems. The larger point is that any of us who work with human beings—especially children—for a living have a compelling ethical need to always use truth in advertising.

A second reason that you do not want to risk misrepresenting the data collected during an FBA also applies if the BIP is not successful. If the BIP is unsuccessful and you are clear and descriptive about how the data were collected, subsequent professionals can build on the work that you started instead of starting over from the beginning. Even if your hypothesis about the function of a target behavior was wrong, the data you collected can still be useful. Building on the work that you started can be a significant time-saver, which is important because, as discussed earlier, we want to effectively intervene as quickly as possible in the developmental process of any behavioral challenge.

Another reason that I like to be as detailed as possible about the strength of data collected during an FBA is that, in ideal circumstances, caregivers or other significant adults in the child's life will have participated in the FBA process. If caregivers are working collaboratively with you to try to change a challenging behavior, you need for them to know if the BIP recommendations are made from weak data. It is not unusual for caregivers to come to school meetings about their child—particularly if behavior problems are involved—to find themselves adrift among a large group of educational professionals. The intent of involving a lot of people with a variety of expertise has the benefit of ensuring that as many disciplines, perspectives, and ideas are focused on solving a problem for a child as possible.

The downside of this arrangement is that it is easy for caregivers to feel outnumbered (especially if they are). Parents who feel outnumbered and intimidated may initially accept recommendations with which they really do not agree, especially if a conference roomful of "experts" made the recommendations. Conversely, other caregivers in this situation may become hostile. Neither of these outcomes fosters effective home–school collaboration, so neither of these states of affairs is in the best interest of the child. We need to be honest; sometimes an opinion offered by an expert is exactly that—an opinion—and people have a right to judge for themselves the value of opinions. This is true even if people do the unthinkable and conclude that your opinion is not necessarily better than theirs because of Waller's Thirteenth Rule of Child Behavior Management: *Opinions, especially concerning the best course of action with a child, are like comfortable old sneakers—we tend to think that everybody's but our own stink.*

The final reason that I think it is important to be honest about the strength of data upon which BIP recommendations are made is that sometimes I like to make recommendations based on weak data relating to factors that may have an impact on the problem behavior. For example, I have consulted in several situations in which a student was engaging in physically aggressive behavior toward other students or teachers, and during interviews with parents I discovered that the child was participating in karate classes. The logic behind this is understandable. Martial arts classes often advertise that they teach children such traits as discipline, patience, and self-esteem.

However, I am aware of no data supporting such statements, and certainly none indicating that children who are physically aggressive to others have stopped initiating physically aggressive behavior as a result of participating in martial arts classes. In fact (and this could just be me here), it seems counterintuitive to provide children who engage in aggressive behavior with hand-to-hand combat training. I think it might be an even better idea to enroll people in anger management classes with marksmanship training. Nothing calms raging fury like busting a few caps in a silhouette target.

A similar finding that I have made on numerous occasions for children exhibiting aggression toward others was that they had ready, if not virtually unfettered, access to violent media entertainment such as movies and video games with a rating inconsistent with their age or developmental level. There are a lot of data available suggesting that exposure to violent movies and violent video games is a bad idea for any child, so I feel quite comfortable, in situations involving student aggression, making the recommendation to restrict access to this type of entertainment.

To accommodate the variable strength that can exist in FBA data, I make recommendations in a tiered format, with first-tier recommendations being based on the strongest data down to third-tier recommendations based on weakest data. I include an explanation of the tiers on my submitted reports. Appendix C provides the format that I use when writing these reports. You can feel free to use it in developing a report format of your own or to use the whole thing in your own work if you would like.

As you can see, the suggestion to restrict access to violent video games can be made as a third-tier recommendation. In my professional opinion, this is an appropriate recommendation to make because the research is absolutely clear that access to these stimuli can have a negative impact on children who aggress against others (and on children who don't as well). However, such a recommendation is not based on cause-and-effect observations and other direct data collected during the FBA. Nonetheless, I think that it is useful to have the latitude to include such recommendations when there is a good likelihood that the target behavior is impacted—avoid opinions and philosophizing.

As an educator, you will sometimes learn of things to which a child in your class is being exposed that, based on research and on your training and experience, you know may be affecting a student in a negative way. The tiered approach to support planning recommendations may provide a means to provide such feedback that is neither overly intrusive nor judgmental. By the same token, you are acknowledging that any recommendations made on such indirect or inferential information involves, at least to some extent, your professional opinion. Caregivers may—or may not—agree with your opinion.

CHAPTER NINE

FBA Within an RTI Framework

A frequent approach that is taken when trying to change undesirable behavior, especially the behavior of children, is to apply consequences. Certainly, the judicious use of consequences (positive or negative) can be powerful tools in changing behavior. One of the advantages of functional behavioral assessment (FBA) and function-based intervention planning, however, is that FBA gives us several points at which we can intervene—antecedent interventions, behavior interventions, teaching interventions, *and* consequence interventions. This book focuses primarily on providing an introduction to antecedent interventions for several reasons. The first reason is the way that I conceptualize behavior supports within a response to intervention (RTI) framework. A thorough description and explanation of RTI is beyond the purview of this book, and you can find innumerable, good references that do the topic justice. I will provide a brief description of how behavior might be conceptualized within an RTI framework.

RTI is a tiered approach to meeting student needs guided by data-based decision making (Figure 9.1). If using a behavioral model of RTI, all students must have access to research-supported strategies—in this case, behavior management strategies. From an RTI approach, all students would be exposed to research-based practices—both teaching practices and behavior management practices. Examples of such research-based universal behavior support strategies would include the Paxis Good Behavior Game

Figure 9.1   Behavior Management Hierarchy Within Response to
Intervention Tiers

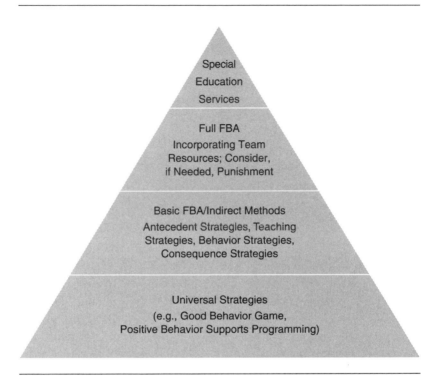

or schoolwide Positive Behavior Supports (PBS) programming. Unfortunately, even when using effective programs like PBS, there are some students who continue to have behavioral challenges even though far fewer students will have such problems.

RTI would require data indicating a lack of progress before you could move to more intensive intervention strategies. Students who continue to struggle behaviorally, even when exposed to research-based behavioral strategies, would need more intense—or tier 2—interventions. Tier 2 behavioral supports could include beginning a basic FBA using several indirect methods and developing a BIP limited to the use of positive interventions. For students who need help beyond tier 2, a collaborative team and an FBA involving at least descriptive analysis and possibly functional analysis could occur on tier 3. For students still failing to progress who continue to need further, specialized help, tier 4 would provide intense intervention options such as special education services.

Students with this level of need require the benefit of an interdisciplinary team. An example of a team-based approach to behavioral problem solving may be found in Appendix D.

Placing a basic FBA and restricting the BIP to use of positive strategies in tier 2 offers unique appeal. First and most obvious, this approach begins with focusing on the function of challenging behavior rather than on presumed personality flaws within the student and reduces the likelihood of causing the frustration and inefficiency of pulling interventions out of the air until you, Mr. Magoo-like, stumble accidentally on something that works.

If, perchance, your basic FBA does not facilitate formulating an accurate hypothesis about the function of a challenging behavior and your interventions are not successful, the data that you have collected can be incorporated into a more sophisticated FBA. Thus, your work—and your time—are not wasted. The emphasis on positive strategies detours the common approach of giving negative consequences following an undesirable behavior. Finally, there is an emphasis on antecedent interventions and on teaching. Effectively implementing antecedent interventions means that you have engaged in primary prevention. In other words, you will have prevented the problem behaviors' occurrence rather than being reactive after undesirable behavior occurs. This is surely the best of possible outcomes.

A WORD ABOUT PUNISHMENT

Am I saying that students in school should never be punished? There are purists of the positive camp who would say punishment should not be used. I am not so pure. Even the PBS approach can incorporate punishment. It is not, however, the first thing tried. Punishment will probably be needed sometimes. I would encourage certain parameters for using punishment.

Don't use punishment first. There are numerous positive approaches that should always be tried before punishment, and these approaches have a very high likelihood of success. Technically, a "punisher" is something following a target behavior that reduces the occurrence of that behavior. There are several techniques in applied behavior analysis that are used to reduce unwanted behavior without using punishment, so why punish first? Don't use punishment without clear acknowledgement of the risks associated with using punishers, and there are several. Punishment won't promote student mental health or school engagement. It can cause avoidance, frustration, and even aggression. You can also cause punishment momentum (my made-up term), which has the opposite effect of behavior momentum. Just like praising a student's attempts to complete math problems can promote and encourage other positive behaviors, punishment tends to stifle all behavior, not just the specific undesirable behavior.

If punishment is to be used, it should be used only with careful observation of cause and effect. If something aversive is being done to a student in the school setting, it should be stopped immediately if it does not actually reduce the target behavior. Punishment, I firmly believe, has negative side effects not just for our students, but for us as well. There is a psychological price tag associated with doing unpleasant things to other people that, in my opinion, contributes to phenomena such as teacher burnout. Finally, placing consideration of punishers in tier 3 means that you have not only brainstormed all possibilities for positive interventions, but that you have gotten the thinking of the team involved. Even if I have run out of ideas, a team member often comes up with a strategy that I didn't consider, and that strategy often works.

CHAPTER NOTES

Phenomenal information about positive behavior approaches is available on the Web. The first place to start is probably http://www .pbis.org/main.htm.

The Paxis Good Behavior Game is an intervention my students and I have used always with positive effect. Research strongly supports it, and it can be implemented on a classwide basis with a small amount of preparation (it can also be used schoolwide); information is available at http://www.paxis.org/.

CHAPTER TEN

A Beginner's Look at Function-Based Support Planning

W e have covered a lot of information and are moving to the purpose of everything discussed before—developing a support plan. Assessment for the sake of assessment is useless. Fortunately, functional behavioral assessment (FBA) is used directly to plan behavior interventions. As was mentioned previously, a behavior intervention plan (BIP) is not, as some think, what we will do to a student whenever they do something undesirable. A BIP is the plan that discusses what we will do differently. Beyond this key point, the BIP is based entirely on the function of the behavior.

ATTENTION

Acquiring attention from others probably accounts for the majority of behavior problems seen in schools. We are social animals— though perhaps some of us dolphins and some of us wart hogs—and we crave social interaction. We must interact with others. We learn how to interact with others in a variety of ways, but one of the strongest ways that we learn to interact with others is by watching others and by imitating behaviors that seem to work well for them. We watch others and we attempt to do similar things. We watch other people engage in social interaction and succeed or fail. Hopefully, we learn from their mistakes. Remember some of the social rules discussed earlier that we have learned and that we follow but rarely if ever think about. How did you learn how much distance you should maintain between yourself and someone with whom you are talking? How did you learn where to look when talking to someone? How did you learn how often you should blink while you are talking to someone? Throughout our lives we are continuously watching others and, with certain exceptions related to you by marriage, we are continuously learning, adjusting, and improving our social performance.

Children *must* be given our attention and nurturance. Unfortunately, not every student will know how to access our attention in ways we desire. Children who cannot get our attention in preferred ways must still access our attention. As a result, some students will get our attention in ways that we don't desire. The pattern of learning to acquire primarily negative attention is accidental. Because no one is perfect, a child will invariably, at some point, do something that requires a correction or mild reprimand. If the child is in a state of attention deprivation when this negative attention is given, we have met the child's need even though our intention may have been to redirect or correct the child.

Even though it starts with a small set of circumstances, a pattern of acquiring negative attention can begin to rapidly build upon itself. Eventually, most of a student's need for attention may be met the opposite of the way that we want her to get our attention. This (believe it or not) is not a bad thing. Teachers must prompt and redirect and provide feedback. Children must get adult attention. It is actually, therefore, a good thing if they *are* getting attention in a way that we don't prefer—because they are getting their needs met.

The consequences of a child not getting her need for attention met are severe, and it's not overstating things to say even life threatening. A state of deprivation, whether it's attention, calories, or sleep, will profoundly affect the behavior of children. Just like you might doze off during a faculty meeting if you are in a state of sleep deprivation—which you would never do under ordinary circumstances because of the constant rivulets of intellectual titillation that flow like water over the falls—a child who is in a state of attention deprivation can, and likely will, behave in ways that resolve her state of deprivation.

HER PLATE IS BIGGER

Furthermore, some children just need more attention than others. Think about it like this: most of us have a body temperature of 98.6 degrees Fahrenheit. But 98.6 degrees is really the average body temperature of homo sapiens. Some people have a body temperature of 99 degrees, and this is perfectly normal for them. Body temperatures, like so many other phenomena, follow a normal distribution (also called a normal curve). Some individuals, in their normal human condition, are cooler than 98.6 degrees and some people are warmer than 98.6 degrees, but most of us fall really close to that number. A few people, though, will be outliers, in that they are not so close as most other people to 98.6 degrees.

In a similar way, some students need more adult attention than other students. Most of them will have similar need levels for your attention, but there will be outliers. It may be inconvenient, but for some students it is normal and necessary. We may be attending to Peanut about the same amount that we are attending to our other students, but he is still in a state of attention deprivation that makes him vulnerable to the acquisition of negative attention. If children are in a state of deprivation, they will get their needs met. Many of your students will appear to have similar needs, but they all actually have different needs and some may have needs markedly disparate from the other children. Resist the urge to say, "But I don't have to do that for my other students," because you know, as a self-actualized highly trained educational professional, that different children have different needs.

Sometimes, of course, students don't want our attention—at least not the way they are getting it. Some people are quite shy and overt attention may be aversive to them. So Peanut is calling out and disrupting class, as Peanut often will. Attention can affect behavior in several ways: A student's behavior may be reinforced by getting attention from an adult or by avoiding attention from an adult *or* her behavior may be reinforced by getting attention from peers or by avoiding attention from peers. Here are some ways that you can begin to distinguish the manner in which attention impacts a target behavior.

Pick a couple of random students in the classroom to serve as a basis for comparison. Count the number of opportunities to respond in class that these two students are given and compare them to Peanut. Covertly, watch Peanut carefully. Do his eyes glance toward the teacher, especially if he is doing something to push a boundary?

If so, you might be tempted to respond, as I have heard many teachers say, that he keeps cutting his eyes at you because Peanut knows exactly what he's doing and he's just trying to push your buttons. Another possible interpretation is that Peanut wants your attention but doesn't know how to go about getting it the way you prefer. Is Peanut more likely to have an adult look at him or talk to him if he is breaking a rule than at other times?

Contemplate teacher proximity. A normal human reaction is for us to tend to avoid people with whom we are in conflict. If Peanut is a classroom "trouble causer," does the teacher still interact with and approach Peanut or does the teacher tend to stay a row or two away? Does she make eye contact with him? If Peanut does begin to engage in disrupting the classroom, does the teacher then use proximity? Consider the ways in which minor behavioral challenges are addressed. If reprimands are used; do they stop, increase, or have no effect on classroom disruptions? If reprimands have no effect on or if they seem to increase the target behavior, acquiring adult attention could serve as a function of the behavior. When considering any student behavior that is undesirable it also may not hurt to remember Waller's Fourteenth Rule of Child Behavior Management: *Adult attention is as surely a physical need as food is, so don't allow a student to starve under your supervision.*

ESCAPE

I understand that there is a show on television that pits the brains of a fully grown adult against those of a fifth-grade school student. I also understand—I don't know—I've never seen the show myself—that the end result of this intellectual clash of titans is that it often turns out to be a real struggle—and sometimes the fifth-grader wins. I can see a couple of ways to interpret this. One way is to make the assumption that we should immediately amend the Constitution of the United States of America by lowering the age at which a person can legally be elected President before us adults, imbeciles that we are, get lost in our living rooms and lurch about in dim-witted circles, hopelessly lost, until we perish from dehydration.

Another way that the results could be interpreted is to assume that the average factoid learned by the average fifth-grader has absolutely no relevance to the life of the average adult. Because the adult never actually uses these factoids in any way, the adult dumps these wasted sound bites from his mind and uses that same brain space for important adult information, such as remembering the names of lead singers from 1980s rock-and-roll bands. Actually, it is possible that there are hundreds of ways to interpret the issue of fifth-graders being smarter than adults but, what with my being an adult, I am simply too stupid to know what they are.

If we have figured out that a lot of the snippets that we learned in school have no importance in our lives, there is at least a decent chance that a lot of school children have figured out that they don't really care about knowing the speed of a train that left New York six hours ago any more than you do. In other words, they are about as excited by some of the content that they are required to learn as you were at the same age. Many children will try to escape from something they find unpleasant, too.

Consider the general classroom environment and the typical student responses to the activity at hand. Are most of the students active, interested, and engaged, or do they seem somewhat unenthusiastic? Do the students seem relatively happy while doing assignments and while within the classroom setting? Does Peanut do very well in physical education but become a behavioral challenge in math? Does Peanut seem to do well with most of his teachers but become blatantly defiant for one or two—even if one of the one or two is you? Is the teacher a person with charisma or would you say that he exudes roughly the same magnetism as a congealed dessert? Has Peanut been sent to time out or to the office for his disruptive behavior? If Peanut was removed from the setting or activity, did the removal stop, increase, or have no effect on his classroom disruptions. Answering each of these questions can facilitate your hearing loudly and clearly what Peanut is telling you about his behavior. Listening carefully might also require you to keep in mind Waller's Fifteenth Rule of Child Behavior Management: *Children experience stress just like we do, so be sensitive to their need to sometimes be given access to a method of flight so that we reduce the chances of having a fight.*

TANGIBLES

Almost every student who draws breath is absolutely bombarded by a wide array of media with temptations for tantalizing trivial trinkets that they should want. Intellectual prime-time television programming is interrupted for seconds at a time, preempting otherwise important educational programming about what we should not wear. These seconds are purchased by corporate conglomerates, many of which spend more money to advertise products that children should want than the amount of money comprising the gross national product of many small countries. These advertisements are extremely sophisticated, researched, and tested for effectiveness so completely that many households around the world—maybe around the universe—actually have a device that can be placed surreptitiously near an unsuspecting person and can, by remote control, be made to emit sounds associated with gastrointestinal dyspepsia. Not surprisingly, children tend to desire things. They do not tend to desire things more than their caregivers or teachers. Having realized that children tend to desire tangible items, many teachers incorporate the use of opportunities to earn tangibles into their classroom management plan.

Conversely, some teachers will not use tangible items of any sort. This group of teachers frequently makes the argument that it will not participate in "bribing" students. However, most definitions of the word bribe that I have seen involve getting someone to engage in illegal behavior for material gain. Interestingly, I have never heard one single teacher in this group call human resources and angrily demand the school system immediately cease sending monthly bribes to their personal bank account. Using tangibles as motivators for students can be a useful part of an effective behavior plan, but if and how they are used is up to you.

Despite the addiction to curios that our society perpetuates, I must say that, among the hundreds of FBAs that we have completed, no one I have worked with has ever seen a child engaging in challenging classroom behavior in which the function of their behavior was clearly and totally obtaining tangibles. In fact, I have only worked with one child for whom taking tangible items from other people seemed to be the function of his behavior, and he met the diagnostic criteria for kleptomania. I am not suggesting that you will never find the function of a challenging school behavior to be acquiring tangibles. There are undoubtedly students who take tangible items simply to have them—behavior also alternatively referred to as stealing or as taxation.

These students, after an ongoing pattern of such behavior has been observed, may meet the diagnostic criteria for conduct disorder—often referred to in school settings as "social maladjustment." I don't provide this information to suggest that the label conduct disorder is helpful in any way as far as changing undesirable behavior. However, students who engage in a pattern of this type of behavior will probably require you to seek assistance from outside the classroom. And think about Waller's Sixteenth Rule of Child Behavior Management: *Research shows that quantity of tangible property is not related to how happy a person is, so tangibles should be a secondary part of your classroom management plan, lying distantly behind things that really do contribute to happiness such as opportunities to be successful.*

A Brief Word on Automatic Reinforcement—Sensory Stimulation

Younger children often engage in behaviors that can be disruptive in the classroom because their deeds are reinforced by sensory stimulation. An example of such behavior in very young children, but that certainly may be seen in early grades, is thumb sucking. Everybody has certain behaviors that are reinforced by sensory input, such as turning-on-the-television behavior. I have seen a variety of behaviors that seemed to occur because of sensory stimulation in the general classroom, and probably the most common of these is pencil tapping (sometimes accompanied by the school chair boogie). Although some teachers are distressed by such behaviors, I have never viewed them as serious. Of course, the severity of these behaviors relates to additional factors, such as your personal level of tolerance. However, some students can engage in very disruptive behaviors that are reinforced by sensory stimulation, such as masturbation and hand mouthing.

If at some point you find yourself in the position of attempting to intervene with behaviors that function to provide sensory stimulation, you are definitely going to want to try antecedent interventions. One piece of prevailing knowledge related to addressing these behaviors after the fact is that you must find alternatives that compete, from a sensory input perspective, with the target behavior in order to change them. This can be easier said than done.

Consider the example of thumb sucking, which is frequently related to sensory input. In order to find sensory input that competes with thumb sucking, it will help you to have an understanding of how much stimulation is associated with thumb sucking. To get a sense for what you are dealing with, it might be useful for you

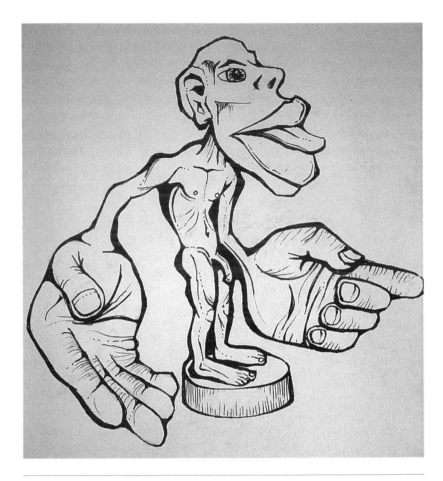

Source: Illustration by Amber Kerr.

to look at the homunculus. The sensory homunculus is a picture representing how much sensory stimulation is involved with corresponding parts of human anatomy. Any resemblance to your cousin is purely coincidental.

Looking at the homunculus, you can see that there is a great deal of innervations dedicated to both the hands and the lips; much more than most people probably realize. One strategy that I have seen used for thumb sucking is the implantation of a dental device that prevents the thumb from being fully inserted in the mouth. There may be research suggesting that this device is effective—I don't know. However, in the cases I have seen involving the use of this dental device by children, it has not resulted in cessation of—or even appreciable reduction of—thumb sucking. Looking at the homunculus, it is easy to see why. Regardless of whether the thumb fits completely in the mouth, a child still receives a *great* deal of sensory stimulation from the hand and lips, even with attempted thumb sucking.

Antecedent interventions are much easier, when they are possible, than trying to find an alternative route to obtaining the amount of sensory input that is experienced by thumb sucking. These types of sensory-related behaviors often occur during periods of low external stimulation. Thus, strategies involved in enriching the environment can greatly reduce the likelihood of behaviors such as thumb sucking.

Alternatively, students may become overstimulated, and the function of some target behaviors is getting a student out of a situation, circumstance, or environment that is too much for them to process and handle at that moment. As an anecdotal note, I have found that sensory issues of this variety are most frequently associated with students who have an autism spectrum disorder, but they are by no means exclusive to students on the autism spectrum.

The pencil-tapping middle-schooler may be acquiring sensory stimulation. Though I have seen behaviors reinforced by sensory stimulation in the general classroom setting, they are, like behaviors that serve the purpose of acquiring tangibles, also relatively infrequent compared with the functions of attention and escape. It also suggests the need to remember Waller's Seventeenth Rule of Child Behavior Management: *If you have ever had trouble focusing your attention during a meeting, in-service, or college class because you need more sensory stimulation than what you are getting listening to or participating in something that someone else thinks is important but that you do not—don't be a hypocrite by having expectations for children more rigorous than what you can do.*

So what does a BIP look like? This is the final, though far from unimportant, benefit to using FBA and BIP: the process provides several different possibilities for intervention. Often, the default response to undesirable behavior in school is to think about giving consequences after the behavior occurs. In fact, a BIP is much more and is best developed to emulate the model in Figure 10.1.

Does this seem like a lot? If you have an evidence-based behavior management plan in place in your classroom or school and you still have a student with a behavioral problem of concern AND we already determined that, in relation to human behavior the best guarantee we

Figure 10.1   Function-Based Intervention Taxonomy

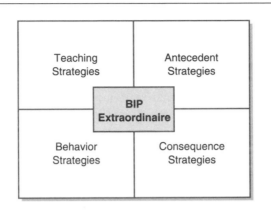

can offer is that we can increase the odds of seeing desired behavior, allow me to ask this question: Do we not owe that student every mechanism of increasing the odds at our disposal? If you think the answer is "yes," as I do, then your BIP will look something like this.

Case Example

Let's return to a previously discussed example of an eighth-grade student identified as having an emotional/behavior disorder who was engaging in out-of-seat behavior associated with disrupting other students when not on task. This behavior was a problem when the student was participating in inclusive general education settings but not during parts of the day when he was in a smaller resource setting. The student (Peanut, of course) also had a hearing impairment and was in possession of a hearing device, but he refused to wear it in school. The target behavior was being out of his seat without permission during class. The definition of *out-of-seat behavior* was a time period of more than five seconds during which there was no contact between the buttocks and the seating surface of the assigned chair during a lesson without permission. *Permission* was defined as raising one's hand and receiving verbal consent from the classroom teacher before getting out of his seat.

After conducting an FBA including indirect assessment and descriptive analysis, you formulated the hypothesis that the function of the target behavior was acquiring adult attention (which is obtained less frequently in the larger general classroom setting) and escape from nonpreferred academic tasks (math in general classroom, which, based on data including work

Figure 10.2   Brief Examples of Domain-Specific Intervention Strategies

Teaching Strategies	• Math skill remediation in smaller group context. • Social skills instruction on appreciating differences and similarities in people, accurate appraisal of the perceptions and intentions of other people. The need for this is based on increased difficulty hearing instruction in larger groups and a desired outcome including wearing his assistive hearing device.
Antecedent Strategies	• Noncontingent adult attention via frequent progress checks, prompts, individual repetition of instruction to ensure hearing and understanding, and instructional assistance during math. • Development of an alternative method of escape via a hand signal communicating the need for teacher assistance. • Peer tutor assistance in regular classroom provided within the context of group work in order to minimize undesirable peer attention.
Behavior Strategies	• Implementation of a self monitoring checksheet to track on-task behavior.
Consequence Strategies	• A simple contingency contract involving the opportunity to earn identified preferred reinforcers based on maintaining a targeted level of on-task behavior. • Identifying a larger reinforcer that is accessible based on wearing the assistive hearing device.

samples, suggests that he is not at the same skill level as peers). The BIP you design based on the data and hypothesis may look something like Figure 10.2.

SUMMARY

In the experience that I have had with FBA, both directly and indirectly, I feel safe in saying that the significant majority, I would say about 85%, of the challenging behaviors that you observe in the classroom will serve the functions of either attention, escape, or a combination of the two. You may see some minor sensory-related behaviors in the general classroom setting, but generally speaking, for significant sensory- and tangibles-related issues, you will probably need help from outside the classroom. At least until you get experience with FBA and BIP. It is extremely important, however, not to make presumptions about the function of a particular classroom behavior before you have completed your FBA. An intervention plan that might work to address getting attention could make an escape-related behavior worse. Whatever the function, the planning process must be guided by Waller's Eighteenth Rule of Child Behavior Management: *The most important word in the phrase "behavior support planning" is "support."*

Conclusion

I hope that you now understand the very basic concepts relating to functional behavioral assessment (FBA) and behavior intervention planning (BIP). If you now get your head around the logic of function-based assessment and planning as it relates to the most common functions of school behavior challenges (attention and escape), you are in an excellent jumping-off point to further more in-depth learning on these topics. I hope that you can see the appeal, both professional and personal, of support planning that is based on what we do differently rather than what we do to students and that while reading this book you have gathered that function-based assessment and intervention is built around the things we do differently. Doing things to students, even if the desired change in behavior is observed, carries unwarranted and undesirable risks to both the students and to you. Everyone will benefit from looking at behavior in a different (and more effective) way.

I hope that you understand the importance of identifying and remediating any skills deficits that exist in order to prevent behavior challenges from occurring and as part of your support planning whenever needed. If your school is working within a response to intervention framework, this will strongly support the ongoing performance of all students and intervening immediately if a skills deficit emerges. Finally, I hope that you can see the utility and the allure of making all possible use of positive behavior supports beginning with the sometimes overlooked antecedent interventions, and that you will not fall into the trap of always thinking of support planning in terms of consequences. In every case possible, I hope you will strategize ways to intervene before the problem actually occurs.

If you share any of these hopes or have experienced any of them as outcomes, this is your introduction to the most effective approach to support planning available. There is a lot to learn about FBA and function-based support planning beyond the material this book covered—even some of the basics were not covered so that the book did not attempt to move beyond its stated purpose—and there are several good books that could serve as your next step in the learning process. Teaching is the most important career you can apply your life to. Although the content children learn from you helps them as they move from challenge to challenge in their lives, it is the way that you approach behavior challenges and the example they see when they watch you adapt to difficult situations that may have the most meaningful impact on their later functioning in everyday life.

CHAPTER NOTES

For those with an interest in learning more about the topic of FBA and BIP and who want to continue to ease into the topic, I would suggest that your next book be:

O'Neill, R. E., Horner, R. H., Albin, R. W., Sprague, J. R., Storey, K., & Newton, J. S. (1997). *Functional assessment and program development for problem behavior.* Boston: Brooks/ Cole.

Anyone interested in really jumping in with both feet might consider:

Sharpe, T. L., & Koperwas, J. (2003). *Behavior and sequential analysis: Principles and practice.* Thousand Oaks, CA: Sage.

Appendix A

Sample Behavioral Assessment Interview—
Student

Student Name: _____ **Age:** _____

Grade: _____ **Date:** _____

Person(s) interviewed: _____

Interviewer: _____

Student Profile: What are the things you like to do, or do well, while at school (activities, classes, helping others, etc.)?

_____

_____

_____

What Would You Work For?

_____

_____

_____

Description of the Behavior

What are some things you do that get you in trouble or that are a problem at school (talking out, not getting work done, fighting, etc.)?

How often do you _____? (insert the behavior listed by the student) *"I get in fights in social studies and science whenever we have to do that stupid group work."*

How long does _____ usually last each time it happens? *"Fights last until the teacher notices. Then I get to leave and just go to the office for a while."*

How serious is _____? (Do you or another student end up getting hurt? Are other students distracted?)

Summarize Antecedent (and Setting Events)

What kinds of things make it more likely that you will have this problem (difficult tasks, transitions, structured activities, small-group settings, teacher's request, particular individuals, etc.)?

When and where is the problem behavior most likely to happen (days of week, specific classes, hallways, bathrooms)?

When is the problem behavior least likely to occur (days of the week, specific classes, hallways, bathrooms)?

Setting events: Is there anything that happens before or after school or in between classes that makes it more likely that you'll have a problem (missed medication, history of academic failure, conflict at home, missed meals, lack of sleep, history of problems with peers, etc.)?

Description of the Consequence

What usually happens after the behavior occurs (what is the teacher's reaction, how do other students react, is the student sent to the office, does the student get out of doing work, does the student get into a power struggle, etc.)?

Source: George Banketas.

Appendix B

Sample Behavior Assessment Summary

Student: _____

School: _____

Age		Referral date	
DOB		Evaluation date	
Grade		Report date	

Target Behavior Definition

Summary of Teacher Interviews

Summary of Parent Interviews

Summary of Student Interviews

Student Preferences

Summary of Record Review

Summary of Data Collection

Hypothesis Statement

Intervention Plan: Antecedent Modification

Intervention Plan: Replacement Behavior(s) and Consequences

Intervention Plan: Response to Target Behavior and Consequences

Evaluation of Intervention Plan

Team Signatures

Source: George Banketas.

Appendix C

Functional Behavioral Assessment Narrative Report

Student Name:

Date:

Brief Introductory Statement:

Target Behavior:

An operational definition of the target behavior developed with caregivers and school personnel.

ASSESSMENT METHODOLOGY

Functional behavioral assessment (FBA) refers to a variety of techniques that may be used to develop hypotheses about the function of a target behavior. If accurate hypotheses about the functions of a target behavior are identified, they can be used to facilitate the development of effective behavior intervention planning. Most practitioners and scholars acknowledge three primary approaches to conducting an FBA: indirect assessment, descriptive analysis, and functional analysis.

Indirect Assessment

Indirect assessment involves a range of approaches to gathering pertinent information on a specified target behavior, including the use of rapid assessment instruments (RAIs), content analysis of school or other germane records, and interviews. Each of these techniques was employed in conducting this FBA.

Rapid Assessment Instruments

Description of any RAIs used, such as the Functional Analysis Screening Tool (FAST) or Problem Behavior Questionnaire (PBQ), who completed them, followed by summary of results.

INTERVIEWS

A detailed summary of interview results for each individual.

OBSERVATIONS

Description of relevant details associated with general observation followed by a brief summary of the observation data.

HYPOTHESIS

My hypothesis regarding the function of the target behavior.

RECOMMENDATIONS

The following recommendations are based on the data collected during the FBA process. They are delineated as first-tier recommendations, second-tier recommendations, and third-tier recommendations. The tiers are provided based on the strength of the evidence upon which the recommendations are based, with first-tier recommendations being based on the strongest evidence and third-tier recommendations based on the weakest available evidence.

First-Tier Recommendations

Recommendations based on a hypothesis of the target behavior confirmed by the results of a functional analysis; or

A hypothesis developed through descriptive analysis and supportive evidence of indirect assessment; or

A hypothesis developed by the convergence of at least three sources of data from indirect assessment and supported by primary source research findings.

Second-Tier Recommendations

Recommendations based on a hypothesis developed through the convergence of at least two sources of indirect assessment and supported by psychological, personality, or educational assessment meeting acceptable requirements for reliability, validity, and other psychometric standards and which have primary source research support; or

Recommendations based on a hypothesis developed through the convergence of two sources of indirect assessment and incorporating diagnostic information from a licensed psychiatrist, psychologist, or clinical social worker and supported by primary source research findings.

Third-Tier Recommendations

Recommendations based on one source of indirect assessment, professional judgment, and supported by primary source research findings; or

Recommendations based on the convergence of one source of indirect assessment and the judgment of other involved professionals with acknowledged expertise in the target behavior, supported by related primary source research findings.

RECOMMENDATIONS

First-Tier Recommendations

Each tier 1 recommendation listed separately, including an explanation of what the recommendation means and implementation issues.

Second-Tier Recommendations

Each tier 2 recommendation listed separately, including an explanation of what the recommendation means and implementation issues.

Third-Tier Recommendations

Each tier 3 recommendation listed separately, including an explanation of what the recommendation means and implementation issues.

CONCLUSION

Any concluding remarks that you think are relevant and should be included in the report.

Source: Raymond J. Waller.

Appendix D

Sample Collaborative Team Activity Guide

SST Phases	PBS Steps	Team-Centered Activities
Initiating	Step 1: Review the referral to SST.	• Prioritize referral behaviors. • Definition of the target behavior. • Interview the teacher(s) where behavior is occurring. • Interview the student. • Record review. • Define team roles and responsibilities. • Team suggests interventions.
Assessment and Planning	Step 2: Conduct a behavior assessment.	Team decides on: • What additional information should be gathered about target behavior? • How information will be gathered (what tool)? • Who conducts behavior assessment for the team?

	Step 3: Develop a hypothesis.	Team will: • Analyze and interpret behavior assessment data. • Agree on hypothesis statement about function (which will guide team-planning efforts).
	Step 4: Develop the support plan.	Team will: • Use the FBA to generate options for antecedent modifications, replacement behaviors, and reinforcers. • Develop action steps for carrying out plan.
Implementing, Evaluating, and Revising	Step 5: Implement, monitor, and evaluate support plan.	Team will: • Determine outcomes to be measured. • Decide on tools to measure outcomes. • Monitor intervention plan to determine if plan is working. • Celebrate, or, • Modify plan, if needed.

SST, student support team; PBS, positive behavior supports; FBA, functional behavioral assessment.

Source: George Banketas.

Bibliography

Aber, J. L., Brown, J. L., & Jones, S. M. (2003). Developmental trajectories toward violence in middle childhood: Course, demographic differences, and response to school-based intervention. *Developmental Psychology, 39,* 324–348.

Alberto P. A., & Troutman, A. C. (2008). *Applied behavior analysis for teachers* (8th ed.). Upper Saddle River, NJ: Prentice Hall.

Anderson, C. A., Berkowitz, L., Donnerstein, E., Huesmann, L. R., Johnson, J. D., Linz, D., Malamuth, N. M., et al. (2003). The influence of media violence on youth. *Psychological Science in the Public Interest, 4,* 81–110.

Barnett, O., Miller-Perrin, C. L., & Perrin, R. D. (2005). *Family violence across the lifespan: An introduction.* Thousand Oaks, CA: Sage.

Beckett, K., & Sasson, T. (2004). *The politics of injustice: Crime and punishment in America.* Thousand Oaks, CA: Sage.

Buhs, E. S., Ladd, G. W., & Herald, S. L. (2006). Peer exclusion and victimization: Processes that mediate the relation between peer group rejection and children's classroom engagement and achievement? *Journal of Educational Psychology, 98,* 1–19.

Burley, R., & Waller, R. J. (2005). Effects of a collaborative behavior management plan on reducing disruptive behaviors of a student with ADHD. *Teaching Exceptional Children Plus, 1*(4), Article 2. Retrieved March 16, 2008, from http://escholarship.bc.edu/education/tecplus/vol1/iss4/art2/

Carr, J. E., & LeBlanc, L. A. (2003). Functional analysis of problem behavior. In W. O'Donohue, J. E. Fisher, & S. C. Hayes (Eds.), *Cognitive behavior therapy: Applying empirically supported techniques in your practice* (pp. 167–175). Hoboken, NJ: Wiley.

Chandler, L. K., & Dahlquist, C. M. (2006). *Functional assessment: Strategies to prevent and remediate challenging behavior in school settings* (2nd ed.). Upper Saddle River, NJ: Pearson Prentice Hall.

Christensen, L., Young, R. K., & Marchant, M. (2004). The effects of a peer-mediated positive behavior support program on socially appropriate classroom behavior, *Education and Treatment of Children, 27,* 199–234.

Coffey, C. E., & Brumback, R. A. (2006). *Pediatric neuropsychiatry.* New York: Lippincott, Williams, & Wilkins.

Cowie, H., Boardman, C., Dawkins, J., & Jennifer, D. (2004). *Emotional health and well being: A practical guide for schools.* Thousand Oaks, CA: Sage.

Crone, D. A., & Horner, R. H. (2003). *Building positive behavior support systems in schools.* New York: Guilford Press.

Glenn, J. H., & Waller, R. J. (2007). Reducing irresponsible talking out during class in a 7th grade student with an emotional/behavioral disorder. *Teaching Exceptional Children Plus, 3*(6), Article 2. Retrieved March 10, 2008, from http://escholarship.bc.edu/education/tecplus/vol3/iss6/art2

Hanley, G. P., Iwata, B. A., McCord, B. E. (2003). Functional analysis of problem behavior: A review. *Journal of Applied Behavior Analysis, 36,* 147–186.

Horner, R. H., Sugai, G., Todd, A. W., & Lewis-Palmer, T. (2000). Elements of behavior support plans: A technical brief. *Exceptionality, 8*(3), 205–215.

Immordino-Yang, M. H., & Damasio, A. (2007). We feel, therefore we learn: The relevance of affective and social neuroscience to education. *Mind, Brain, and Education, 1,* 3–10.

Kazdin, A. E. (2001). *Behavior modification in applied settings* (6th ed.). Belmont, CA: Wadsworth.

Muuss, I. B., Bunge, S. A., & Gross, J. J. (2007). Automatic emotion regulation. *Social and Personality Psychology Compass, 1,* 146–167.

Mueller, M. M., & Jeffery, D. J. (2005, April). Assessment and treatment of aggression in a classroom evoked by coughing. Poster presented at the 37th Annual Convention, National Association of School Psychologists, Atlanta, GA.

Mueller, M. M., & Kafka, C. (2006). Assessment and treatment of object mouthing in a public school classroom. *Behavioral Interventions, 21,* 137–154.

Mueller, M. M., Sterling-Turner, H. E., & Moore, J. W. (2005). Towards developing a classroom-based functional analysis condition to assess escape-to-attention as a variable maintaining problem behavior. *School Psychology Review, 34,* 425–431.

O'Neill, R. E., Horner, R. H., Albin, R. W., Sprague, J. R., Storey, K., & Newton, J. S. (1997). *Functional assessment and program development for problem behavior.* Boston: Brooks/Cole.

Repp, A. C., & Horner, R. H. (1999). *Functional analysis of problem behavior: From effective assessment to effective support.* Albany, NY: Wadsworth.

Seligman, M. E. P. (1994). *What you can change and what you can't: The complete guide to successful self-improvement.* New York: Alfred A Knopf.

Seligman, M. E. P. (1995). *The optimistic child: A proven program to safeguard children against depression and build lifelong resilience.* New York: Harper Collins.

Seligman, M. E. P. (2002). *Authentic happiness: Using the new positive psychology to realize your potential for lasting fulfillment.* New York: Free Press.

Sharpe, T., & Koperwas, J. (2003). *Behavior and sequential analysis: Principles and practice.* Thousand Oaks, CA: Sage.

Sheldon, K. M., & Lyubomirsky, S. (2007). Is it possible to become happier? (And if so, how?) *Social and Personality Psychology Compass 1,* 129–145.

Swets, J. A., Dawes, R. M., & Monahan, J. (2000). Psychological science can improve diagnostic decisions. *Psychological Science in the Public Interest, 1,* 1–26.

Taylor, R. L. (1990). *Distinguishing psychological from organic disorders: Screening for the psychological masquerade.* New York: Springer Publishing Company.

Waller, R. J. (Ed.). (2006). *Fostering child and adolescent mental health in the classroom.* Thousand Oaks, CA: Sage.

Waller, R. J. (2008). *The educator's guide to solving common behavior problems.* Thousand Oaks, CA: Corwin Press.

Waller, R. J., Lewellen, K., & Bresson, D. (2005). The debate surrounding psychotropic medication usage in young children. *School Social Work Journal, 29,* 53–61.

Wilder, D. A., & Carr, J. E. (1998). Recent advances in the modification of establishing operations to reduce aberrant behavior. *Behavioral Interventions, 13,* 43–59.

Williams, K. D. (2007). Ostracism: The kiss of social death. *Social and Personality Psychology Compass, 1,* 236–247.

WEB SITES

Collaborative for Academic, Social, and Emotional Learning: http://www.casel.org/home.php

A drawing of the licking apparatus used to test the Tootsie Pop dilemma can be found at http://www.tootsie.com/gal_machine.php

National Center for Learning Disabilities: http://www.ncld.org/index.php?option=content&task=view&id=598

OSEP Technical Assistance Center on Positive Behavioral Interventions and Supports: www.pbis.org

Index

CORWIN PRESS

The Corwin Press logo—a raven striding across an open book—represents the union of courage and learning. Corwin Press is committed to improving education for all learners by publishing books and other professional development resources for those serving the field of PreK–12 education. By providing practical, hands-on materials, Corwin Press continues to carry out the promise of its motto: **"Helping Educators Do Their Work Better."**